Civil Wars, Child Soldiers and Post Conflict Peace Building in West Africa

Edited by
Amadu Sesay

ISBN: 978-2194-27-1
ISBN-13: 978-978-2194-27-5

© AFSTRAG 2003

Published by College Press and Publishers Ltd

This Book was published with support from Ford Foundation

About the International Strategic and Peace Research Group (AFSTRAG)

The African Strategic and Peace Research Group (AFSTRAG) was established in 1992 as an independent non-governmental, non-political, non-profit making action-oriented research organisation. Its aim is to provide a platform for analyzing strategic issues, particularly those relating to peace and security, and their effects on the political, military, socio-economic and human conditions in Africa.

Its membership is made up of eminent scholars, senior military officers, public servants, business executives and other persons with interests and proven capacity for research and intellectual discourses on African affairs. The members are motivated by the perceived need to provide an African perspective to the search for solutions to the problems of human security, peace and stability and the social and economic conditions on the continent.

Some Recent Publications by AFSTRAG

1. **Conflict Management Mechanism in West Africa**, edited by Olu Adeniji, 1997.
2. **Civil Society, Good Governance and Security in Africa**, edited by R. A. Akindele, Vantage Publishers, Ibadan, 2003.
3. **Civil Society and Ethnic Conflict Management in Nigeria**, edited by Thomas A. Imobighe, Spectrum Books, Ibadan, 2003.
4. **Data Base on Peace and Security in West Africa**, edited by Ishola Williams, Kwame Nkrumah University, Kumasi, 2003

Contents

List of Tables

Appendices

Acknowledgements

This project started as a dream in 1997 when a group of researchers and scholars-Professor Tom Imobighe, Professor Emeka Nwokedi of blessed memory, Professor Celestine Bassey, Dr. Jimi Adisa and Mr. L. S. Aminu-met in Ile-Ife, Osun State, for three days under my chairmanship to put together their thoughts on some of the burning issues in Nigeria and West Africa then. At that time, two ferocious and rather uncivilized wars were raging in two countries on the West Coast of Africa, that in Liberia which started in December 1989, and the other one in Sierra Leone which broke out less than two years later in March 1991. After three hectic days of brainstorming, they came out with several ideas and "documents" which subsequently formed the basis of proposals sent to the Ford foundation's West Africa office in Lagos for possible funding. One of the proposals was on "Civil Wars, Child Soldiers and Post Conflict Reconstruction in West Africa". The choice of the topic for the proposal reflected then the concern of the researchers as well as developments in West Africa, for the sub-region was going through some of its most difficult period since the flush of independence in the late 1950s. Arising from that was the phenomenon of children who were being used as soldiers in both Liberia and Sierra Leone and the notoriety that had acquired not only for their daring actions in the two wars but also for the large scale atrocities that they were involved in.

While a lot of media attention was focused on their activities in the war front, not much empirical research had been done on the circumstances that led to their involvement in the wars, or how they could be reintegrated into post war civil society in the two countries. There was also a lot of media coverage of the humanitarian emergencies unleashed on the sub-region as a result of the wars, and the efforts of the Economic Community of West Africa States, ECOWAS and the international community to come to grips with the situation. Finally, there was very little attention on post conflict reconstruction, since all efforts were geared towards bringing the wars to an end. Thus, the proposal anticipated several important developments, which would later seize the attention of the sub-region and the rest of the world. It is to the credit of the Ford Foundation then, that even at such an early stage, it was able to fund the project. I would therefore like to seize this opportunity to express our profound gratitude to the Ford Foundation for the project, and now the book. AFSTRAG would like to place on record its appreciation and thanks to the then West Africa Representative, Dr. Akwasi Aidoo for supporting the project. Our thanks also go to Dr. Christine Wing of the New York Office, for her support and encouragement.

My sincere thanks also go to the scholars who participated in this project, for without their commitment, and determination, the project would have remained a pipe dream. I would also like to acknowledge the contribution of, and pay warm tribute to AFSTRAG's Director of Research, Professor R. A. Akindele for being such a nice gentleman and effective overall coordinator. Without his tact, patience, encouragement, and motivation, the researchers would not have been able to see this and other projects through successfully. The staff at the AFSTRAG Secretariat in Lagos also deserve some mention and recognition for their timely reminders and warm hospitality. Finally, I would like to thank all members of my family who, as usual, had to put up with my erratic work habits to ensure the completion of this project and book. Without their understanding and encouragement at all stages of the project, it would have been impossible to complete it within the project period.

I sincerely thank you all.

Section One: Introduction

Chapter One: Introduction
Amadu Sesay and Wale Ismail

1.1 Introduction

The collapse of communism in the late 1980s and the subsequent withdrawal of the great powers from Africa had a very devastating impact on the continent. For it led to the break-down of central political authority, law and order in several states leading in some instances to outright state collapse[1]. One of the sub-regions most affected was West Africa where two bitter and protracted civil wars were fought in Liberia, 1989-1997, and Sierra Leone, 1991-2002. Some of the most distinctive features of these wars were not only their protracted nature, but also the massive use of small arms and light weapons and the involvement of thousands of children as scouts, combatants and rear guards in conflicts. This was particularly so in Sierra Leone under the regime of former military dictator Valentine Strasser and in Liberia where the long period of internecine conflict produced what amounted to a martial culture among youths. This was in spite of the fact that both countries were signatories to several Conventions protecting the rights of the child, such as the African Charter on the Right of the African Child. Another disturbing feature of the wars was the massive atrocities that were committed by all sides and especially by child soldiers. This was particularly so in Sierra Leone where there was rampant amputation of limbs by the rebel Revolutionary United Front, RUF.

The civil wars in Liberia and Sierra Leone posed serious challenges to the international community while they lasted. Nonetheless, it took several years before they were formally brought to an end. Unfortunately, at the time of writing in 2003, Liberia had degenerated once more into civil war, causing untold hardship to hundreds of thousands of its citizens many of whom had either been displaced once again, or had fled to neighbouring

3

States and became refugees. Besides, the situation in Liberia and Sierra Leone also seriously threatened sub-regional peace and stability in West Africa, as well as its economic integration organization, the Economic Community of West African States, ECOWAS, in the absence of focused attention from the United Nations and the great powers. It was the widespread atrocities committed by all sides in the two wars that finally gingered the international community into limited action in the two countries resulting in several halting peace processes and eventually, the end of the two wars. Significantly, the international community demonstrated its disapproval of the atrocities committed during the wars especially those in Sierra Leone, when it set up a war crimes tribunal to try those alleged to have committed crimes against humanity during the civil war in that country.[2]

1.2 Statement of the Problem

Dramatic changes in warfare in the later part of the 20th Century aligned with a rising wave of internal conflicts has brought into prominence the factor of increased participation of children in recent conflicts (see Chapter Three for details). The involvement of "kids" in modern combat poses a severe challenge to prevalent moral norms and legal regulations guiding conduct of modern warfare. More significantly, the rising number of children and their direct involvement has inherent short and long-term implications for the development of children in the affected countries and the society at large (see Chapter Five for details on post war trauma and its management). In particular, the nature of the conflicts has had crucial implications not only for their successful management, but also for effective post-conflict reconstruction and peace building in Liberia and Sierra Leone. This has been a particularly thorny issue in Liberia where the post war regime of Charles Taylor was never able to transform itself from a rebel regime into a national one responsible and answerable to all Liberians.

Unfortunately, however, these issues have been overshadowed and even submerged by concern for children and atrocities associated with their involvement in conflicts by the international community. While that is fine, what has not been addressed by sub-regional leaders and the international community at large is the fact that without an effective programme of post-conflict reconstruction and peace building, it would be difficult to end violence and even atrocities against innocent people, as well as impunity on that part of governments in the two countries. In extreme cases, as in Liberia, the fragile peace fabric totally collapsed, leading once again, to full scale civil war and untold human suffering (see Chapter Three in this volume for details) The implication of this development is that a "potential time bomb" may be ticking continuously even in Sierra Leone as "kids with guns" are re-circulated into normal societies and communities with little or no re-orientation, and into an atmosphere of pervasive want, deprivation and increasing crimes. In that regard, it is important to note here that one of the reasons for the relapse of Liberia into full scale civil war less than five years after the tortuous peace processes brought the war to an end in 1997, was that the reluctance of donors to provide money for disarmament and reintegration programmes simply threw thousands of traumatized and violent children back into the streets. In many cases, these former child combatants maintained close links with former rebel commanders, and were therefore easy to recruit for the new round of civil war.

Several research questions therefore begged for answers. Is there any relationship between the nature of civil war and post conflict reconstruction? What is the impact of post war regimes on post war reconstruction and peace building in collapsed states like Liberia and Sierra Leone? What are the implications; short, medium and long term-for post war reconstruction and peace building given the large number of former child combatants in Liberia and Sierra Leone? Is there a relationship between the responses of the international donor community and effective peace building and reconstruction in post conflict societies? If the answer is yes, what have been the experiences of Liberia and Sierra Leone? Answers to these and several other important questions constitute the research problematique of the study.

1.3 Select Review of the Literature on Child Soldiering

There has been a phenomenal growth in the literature on child soldiers since the 1990s following the unprecedented eruption of violence and civil wars in many parts of the world in the aftermath of the end of East-West ideological rivalries: especially in Europe and Africa. For analytical convenience, however, the review is divided into four broad categories or sections as follows:

a) Child Soldiering in Global Perspectives
b) Child Soldiering in Africa
c) Child Soldiering in West Africa
d) Child Soldiering and the Security Threat Thesis

a) Child Soldiering in Global Perspectives

This section reviews orthodox thoughts and writings on the recruitment and emergence of child soldiers with a view to providing a comprehensive understanding of the phenomenon. Following the horrifying pictures of children bearing arms, the UN General Assembly pursuant to resolution 48/157, instituted the Expert Study on the Impact of Armed Conflict on Children in 1993. The result was the 1996 Graca Machel Study[3], which has since become the basis of global action on the phenomenon of child soldiering. For instance, the creation of the Office of the Special Representative of the UN Secretary General on Armed Conflicts and Children (SRUNSGCAC) was a direct recommendation of the Machel study. The Report noted grimly, that armed conflicts in many parts of the world have turned into attacks on children, and it was shocking that thousands of young people are cynically exploited as combatants. Moreover, Olara Otunnu (SRUNSGCAC), in his report to the UNGA, noted that children were increasingly specially targeted, recruited as combatants or abducted as sex slaves. He puts the number of child soldiers at 300,000 spread across more than 32 countries.[4] Global initiatives on child soldiering have been augmented by the formation of the Coalition Against the Use of Child Soldiers (CAUCS) by child rights groups and non-governmental organizations.

However, in spite of this global reaction and the energetic role of the UN Security Council since 1999 in passing 7 resolutions, 37 debates, and 6 presidential statements condemning the use of children as child soldiers in war[5], the practice continues to challenge policy makers and advocacy groups due to its seeming intractability since the early 1990s. This disturbing report card tasks researchers to reconsider orthodox thoughts on the subject matter in order to enhance its understanding.

While the Machel study provided a necessary point of departure in researches linked to child soldiering, it fails to adequately distinguish between different classes of child soldiers. Although subsequent studies have exposed the use of children as soldiers in Western states such as United Kingdom, United States, etc., yet, this disclosure has had little impact in promoting the systematic understanding of child soldiering globally.

The first distinction that needs to be made involves child soldiers within and outside conflict situations. By clearly separating the contexts of child soldiering, valuable opportunities for investigating the common or different factors responsible for putting children under arms are created. Although this study focuses on the use of child soldiers in theatres of conflict, the categorization along contexts is necessary given the need to avoid the generalization prevalent in existing literature and the possibility of explaining differences or "sameness" in the experiences of child soldiers in war ridden developing countries such as Angola, Guatemala, Peru, Philippines, Sierra Leone, Sri-Lanka, Sudan, etc., and relatively peaceful states like the UK, USA or Luxembourg, among others.

The second category is that of child soldiers found within national armed forces, institutional child soldiers, on the one hand and those within non-state armed groups, non-institutional child soldiers such as private armies or mercenaries, on the other. Although the 2000 Optional Protocol to the 1989 Convention on the Rights of the Child (CRC), Article 18 of the Rome Statute and the International Labour Organization (ILO) statute 182

7

set eighteen years as the minimum age for soldiering, as well as the outlawing of the conscription of children in most states, the continued presence of child soldiers within the ranks of government, pro-government and opposition forces in countries like Guatemala, Peru and Sierra Leone provides a logical basis for this categorization.

The third class of child soldiers focuses on their roles. Here, two groups-active combat and support child soldiers-could be discerned. The former involves child soldiers deployed to the frontline in any capacity such as combatants, human spies or baits, food and ammunition carriers, and mine sweepers. Conversely, the second group of child soldiers refers to children used by armed groups in war support roles such as domestic servants, errand boys, cooks, 'comfort troops', and bodyguards. This categorization is not an attempt to measure the military value of each group since in certain instances, war-support activities may be vital to military success as much as active combat roles. Rather, it is simply an attempt to put important practical and policy issues in clearer analytical perspectives. For instance, in creating the active and support typologies, the existing legal contention over the direct/indirect dichotomy is better understood.[6] Accordingly; the categories have important academic, policy/legal and practical usefulness.

Although a thin line separates the two groups as child soldiers could be used interchangeably in both roles, it is still important to note the differences and their implications for post-conflict political stability and security. For instance, while orthodox writings argue that the overall experiences of child soldiers are negative, this study introduces variations in the degree of negative experiences depending on wartime roles, based on the categorization presented above. Thus, the experiences of active child soldiers are bound to be significantly different from those of support child soldiers due to their deployment to combat positions, and in terms of their exposure to dangers, the use of confidence enhancing drugs, traumatization and degree of alienation from the larger society.

Moreover, the study tries to construct a possible pattern of use by arguing that age (i.e. younger and older child soldiers) and physique, domestic skills such as cooking ability, and operational needs, are possible criteria used in assigning child soldiers to either active or support roles. Thus, the older a child soldier is, the greater are the chances of his being used in active capacities.

b) Child Soldiering in Africa

The presence of over 120,000 child soldiers including five-year olds, spread across 13 states in Sub-Saharan Africa[7] has drawn noticeable dispositions within orthodox thoughts linking the child soldiering to the continent's pre-colonial traditions. The so-called "Africanised" arguments stress that the existence of over 40% of global estimates[8] of child soldiers including the active uses of children who are mostly in their pre-teenage years, is not a mere coincidence, rather, it points to its possible age-long popularity in the region.

Mike Wessels, a leading child psychologist, argues that the definition of "childhood" according to African culture, supports child soldiering for "many African societies regard a 14-year-old boy as a man if he has participated in the traditional rites of passage"[9] and thus eligible for military service. Equally, a child-focused NGO has claimed that "...in Africa, children of 14 are already adults...boys of 14 would automatically be combatants."[10] Evidence from a pre-colonial history of military slavery in Sudan[11] and youth warriors among the Zulus in Southern Africa were used to support this claim.

However, and from a sociological perspective, Bennet has argued that to convincingly construct an "Africanist" argument would involve first, answering the question, is there clear evidence of a constant uniform use of children in combat roles in Africa? If such tradition did indeed exist, was it perpetuated into modern times or was it recreated to serve new and contemporary purposes? Any argument resting on cultural traditions would

9

need to assert something more than the chance occurrence of a particular activity or its fleeting popularity in some country or countries in pre-colonial Africa, for it to be empirically valid. This is important because tradition, in the strict sense, implies that the activity was institutionalized in the sense that it was persistent and widely approved.[12]

The prevalence of child soldiers in contemporary Africa can be linked to the pervasive conflicts in the region. The presence of nearly half of the global estimates of child soldiers in Africa parallels the prevalence of conflict in the region. Between 1960 and 1980, 8 civil wars were fought on the continent; 10 more occurred in the next decade. Between 1960 and 1990 Africa's conflicts accounted for more than 6.5million deaths.[13] In 1999 alone, sub-Saharan Africa accounted for 11 of 27 violent conflicts in the world, equivalent to 40% of total global estimates.[14] The volatility of the African region has been compounded by a population structure in which under 18-year-olds account for over half of its 600m people, the largely ageing population in regions like Europe and Asia, increases the prospects for child soldiering in Africa.

More importantly, perhaps, is the fact that the wars are of an internal nature-that is within states-tends to also facilitate the use of children as soldiers. Not unexpectedly, therefore, the wars in Angola, Liberia, Mozambique, Sierra Leone and Sudan, for instance, involve the pervasive use of children in both active and support roles. The link between the nature of war and use of children as soldiers, albeit in varying degrees of intensity, is equally noticeable in non-African theatres of war; for instance, the civil wars in Afghanistan, Chechnya., El Salvador, Guatemala, Sri Lanka, and Peru.[15]

Bennet has contended that tradition is used to preserve a culture and for gaining moral authority in the community or society. Culture, he adds, is also socially constructed. Finally, culture and tradition are both used by a people to preserve their distinctiveness. Accordingly, if child soldiering is truly African, why did majority of African states sign existing laws prohibiting child soldiering? The continent not only instituted its own Charter on the Rights and Welfare of the Child (1991), it was also the first to 'unequivocally' make eighteen years the minimum age for soldiering.[16] African states have equally adopted several other resolutions including the Yaounde Resolution (1996), Maputo Declaration (1999) and Accra Declaration (2000), are all action plans for the eradication of child soldiering in Africa. The African thesis is not tenable. Although Bennet conceded that children, as part of all available capabilities, could have been used in pre-colonial African societies for military purposes but that was only in acts of self-defence[17] More over, the use of children in such circumstances does not constitute an institutionalized practice. Even when children were inducted into combat groups for offensive purposes, it would be a matter of deliberate policy not institutional.[18]

Furley submits that Africa's social organization is marked with age-grades, where movement from one grade to the next is generally accompanied by a 'rite de passage', a ritual display that focuses public attention on changes in status. When initiates eventually emerge, they are deemed to have shed attributes typical of childhood such as dependency, confinement to family domain and, would have gained some qualities of adulthood such as puberty or cultural identities. Thus he concludes that the Masai warriors, for example, had to wield an extremely heavy spear, which required a man's strength to throw it.[19]

Bennet and Honwana further argue that adulthood was characterized mostly by enrolment in the military age sets. Although the warriors of pre-colonial African armies would not have attained complete adult status, children (under 18-years) were not recruited into regiments nor did they bear arms[20]. In most cases, men were drafted into regiments 3 or 4 years after puberty, and girls were never used as combatants in Africa.[21] In rare cases, children only gave incidental support as non-combatants. Such practice was also discernible in non-Africa societies as well. For instance, the use of

11

children in warships as ratings and drummer boys in Europe, the use of 12 year-olds in Napoleon's army and in Nelson's navy, or the 15 year-olds at the battle of Jutland.[22] The fact that Europe, Asia, North America and Latin America account for the remaining 60% of global estimates for child soldiers suggests child soldiering could not have been exclusively African, even if it were ever present in pre-colonial Africa.

The involvement of children in the Kamajor Civil Defence Force (CDFs) in Sierra Leone provides a practical test for the Africanized argument. Child soldiers are estimated to account for 25% of the CDFs' troop strength.[23] Rather than any cultural inclination, CDFs' use of children ricocheted from the revival of the ancient esoteric Mende cult of invincible and heroic hunting tradition as a communal militia. Encouraged by the Kamajor CDF, displaced civilian groups nominated and sponsored many of their children for training and initiation into CDFs. The voluntary enlistment of child soldiers with the CDFs should therefore be understood more as a function of the "child's ecology"[24] and less as an ideological inclination or cultural practice since it was traditionally a hunting institution, that was only revived as a fighting sect due to wartime exigencies. RUF rebels were seen as *dambi* -animals - preying on the Mende land, and were to be hunted down to protect the community.[25]

Honwana on the other hand, argues that child soldiering is a consequence of colonialism in Africa.[26] It first manifested in the use of children by liberation movements as part of available human resources then for attaining self-government.[27] Angola, Mozambique and South Africa recorded the first large-scale use of children in the 1970s. Moreover, those African states that peacefully negotiated independence were devoid of child soldiering in the early post-independence period due to the unifying effect of "independence nationalism". However, the fragile national consensus in many independent African states, due largely to colonial amalgamation of different ethnic groups into a single state, and compounded by post-independence neocolonial and shadow state[28] practices resulted in serious and protracted crises including civil wars later.

These wars, mostly internal, inevitably generated child soldiers. Child soldiering, she therefore concluded, has to be understood within the context of the crisis of the post-colonial African state. The shifting role of children from the image of the independent child, indicators of family's wealth and sources of future security to killers, is intrinsically linked to the breakdown of society's structure and morality in war-torn independent African states such as Somalia, Sudan, Sierra Leone, Liberia, and Angola. Moreover, states recruiting children into their armed forces have been noticed to be either internally threatened or suspicious of external subversion such as Ethiopia was in the 1980s under the Mengistu regime.[29] From the preceding discussion, it is logical to assert that child soldiering is a function of modern times rather than a fall out from Africa's pre-colonial traditions; child soldiering is 'analogous' to conflicts in sub Saharan Africa especially in the post cold War era.

c) Child Soldiering in West Africa

The outbreak of armed insurgencies in Liberia and Sierra Leone in 1989 and 1991 respectively, not only earned West Africa the unenviable tag of the most volatile sub-region in the 1990s, but equally generated thousands of child soldiers. The conflict in Liberia is supposed to have produced an estimated 20,000 child soldiers while Sierra Leone had 10,000.[30] These figures combined, equal 10% and 25% of total estimates for the SSA and the rest of the world respectively. In addition, while child soldiers in Liberia became cannibals, those in Sierra Leone are associated with the horrendous and highly unusual atrocity of hacking off limbs, severance of ears and buttocks. These appalling pictures and practices challenge us to reconsider the underlying factors responsible for the involvement of children in elite power struggles. It is against this background that this study introduces the role of the contagion effects in the production of child soldiers in the civil wars in Liberia and Sierra Leone.

13

The 1996 Machel study, re-echoing Goodwin-gill and Cohn (1994), noted two forms of recruitment of child soldiers-forced or voluntary. Forced recruitment involves raids, press-ganging, kidnapping or conscription of children for institutional and non-institutional child soldiering. Here unaccompanied children or those in schools, orphanages, refugee camps and other children-centred places are usually vulnerable targets. On the other hand, voluntary recruitment includes the personal decision of children to enlist for service in either national or rebel forces. In most instances, however, girls were forcibly seized because of their gender based sexual services, although there were also reported cases of sodomy. The boy child soldier although coerced in some instances, still enjoyed relative freewill in deciding whether to enlist or not.

Recruitment in Liberia and Sierra Leone took both forms. *Human Rights Watch* in its independent study of child soldiering in the two countries noted that children either voluntarily enlisted or were randomly coerced by all sides in the civil wars.[31] This assertion has been corroborated by studies carried out by Groves (2000), Brett and McCalin (2000). Children joined the NPFL and ULIMO factions in Liberia, and the Kamajor CDFs voluntarily. Although the ability of children whose opinions are unformed and uninformed, to objectively understand and evaluate the risks and advantages involved in bearing arms has been contested, Machel has argued that it is misleading to consider such action as voluntary, for their choice was not exercised freely. Besides, children are also naturally vulnerable because of their emotional and physical immaturity. However, inquiries into the social, economic, political and other influences that make soldiering attractive to children provide valuable insights into their decision to enlist.

The emergence of child soldiers in Liberia and Sierra Leone could be linked to the outbreak of war, as there were no pre-war cases of child soldiering in both countries. Moreover, the seeds of child soldiering are 'analogous' to the causes of the war and had been planted in the pre-war years. State 'dysfunctionism' produced an inherent disposition to child soldiering. This was subsequently augmented by wartime situations. Internal social, economic, military and political factors account for the former, while insecurity and military manpower needs explain the latter. Yet external factors of weaponry and contagion effects complemented the internal tendency towards child soldiering.

The pre-war 'shadow state' and political oppression by Doe in Liberia and Momoh in Sierra Leone, produced internal vulnerabilities that were subsequently exploited by the NPFL and RUF insurgents respectively. The pre-war socio-economic conditions had resulted in high unemployment, high drop out rates due to disruptions in education, hyperinflation and poverty. These developments led to large pools of restless, unemployed and barely educated children who were easily exploited as soldiers.

Moreover, the political alienation of certain groups by the incumbents of power and the desire of such groups for change in their favour, increased local support for insurgents and local militia forces in the two countries. For instance, pre-war victimization of the Gios and Manos by the Doe regime and the reckless counter-insurgency operations of the AFL contributed to the initial massive child volunteers from the Gio and Mano ethnic groups. Children from those groups joined the NPFL either as a survival strategy, to avenge the killing of parents, family members, friends and surrogate parents or to protect themselves and their families from further harassment.[32] Nine-year-old Martin said: "I became a soldier to avenge the death of my father...I came home one day to find him dead and my school down".[33] Abdullah and Muna identified similar factors in explaining Mende support for the civil defence forces in Sierra Leone, even though the CDFs later emerged as pro-government factions.[34]

Furley noted that children became soldiers in Liberia and in Sierra Leone, in part because of the prospects of personal socio-economic and political gains through looting, rape, access to power through the gun and a chance to influence the events that were affecting their lives. The pre-war poor economic conditions in both countries had also denied most children access to basic necessities including education, food and security. Their fate was further compounded by the wartime deprivations; the gun became a symbol of access to scarce food and a new social status of "respectability" in a highly unpredictable environment. The informal decoration of child soldiers with various ranks according to the severity of the atrocities committed by them, as a form of reward system by factions in Liberia and Sierra Leone is a poignant example that supports this contention.

Ideological conviction played a negligible role in the decision of children to enlist in both cases. Factions in both Liberia and Sierra Leone exhibited no clear-cut ideology nor were their wartime-undisciplined behaviour indicative of any superior "philosophy" other than greed for political power and material wealth. The dominant NPFL and other factions in Liberia looted their respective areas of occupation. The RUF/AFRC allies in Sierra Leone massively pillaged the diamond reserves of Sierra Leone in the Kono and Tongo mines during their occupation of those areas. In Liberia children joined the factions because of promises of $5 and pairs of Levi's blue jeans[35] from faction leaders or their representatives. The *San San* boys and children in the *Potes* equally enlisted with the RUF in Sierra Leone because of perceived greater security as well as for prospects of participating in informal economic activities like illegal diamond mining which was very rampant in RUF/AFRC controlled areas.[36]

Additionally, the stalemate factor identified by Machel also influenced the involvement and extensive use of children in the two civil wars. The prolongation of war in the two countries, the high casualty rates and the attendant manpower needs inevitably forced all factions in Liberia, the RUF/AFRC and SLA in Sierra Leone to coerce children into playing active roles in the wars. Alternatively, Goodwin-gill and Cohn have argued that insecurity, a feeling of helplessness and the need to avoid being trapped, are some of the more serious considerations that tilted in favour of the voluntary enlistment of children[37] during the war. They cited as an example, the recruitment of children by the Kamajor CDFs in Sierra Leone.

Cultural explanations for child soldiering are absent in the two case studies. Although *Lofans* in Liberia and *Mendes* in Sierra Leone had warrior histories[38] the historical use of children was clearly absent in the two groups. The recruitment of child soldiers by the CDFs in Sierra Leone should therefore be seen as wartime 'exigency' rather than a manifestation of pre-war history or cultural disposition. It should be pointed in that regard that the *kamajor* is a traditional hunter sect, which metamorphosed into a fighter sect because of the wartime security needs of the people.

The recruitment of child soldiers in the Liberian and Sierra Leonean civil wars was also facilitated by the widespread use of light, inexpensive weapons-the AK47s, AK48s, Kalashinkovs that require no physical prowess or technical expertise to manipulate.[39] The proliferation of light weapons occasioned by the loosely regulated nature of the international arms market especially since the end of the Cold War in1990, has made them easily affordable to factions because of the cheap price of an AK47 ($5), or the equivalent of the price a goat or chicken in sub-Saharan Africa,[40] although the price tends to vary from one country to another.

However, as Ismail has rightly noted, existing literature fails to investigate the role of the contagion effects[41] in the phenomenon of child soldiers in Liberia and Sierra Leone, in spite of its importance, which has been clearly demonstrated in this study. Indeed, the contagion effects can be observed at two levels- precedence and geography. The first relates to the known use of child soldiers in other or earlier theatres of war and the impact of such as a 'ready made example' for subsequent recruitment of children for the war efforts either voluntarily or coercively. It is logical to assert that this factor could influence a group's decision to forcibly recruit children or accept them as volunteers. A child's knowledge of the role played by children in other theatres of war could also influence his decision to enlist or not to enlist voluntarily. While little documented evidence exists to back up this assertion, the very nature of most armed groups or factions makes it rather difficult for them not to accept children in their ranks.[42]

In fact, most rebel groups begin with very small numbers of fighters and usually increase in size as they acquire territories, other spoils of war, or as they gain local acceptability. Expectations of subsequent involvement of children in the war or conflict cannot therefore be ruled out of the groups' initial decisions to launch the first attack. This is more so when the ability of adults to either flee conflict areas or objectively analyze events is better than children are considered. The point that is being made here is that the use of child soldiers by government forces and armed rebel groups in Angola, Ethiopia, Mozambique, Uganda, South Africa and Sudan in the 1980s did contribute directly and indirectly to the surge in child soldiering in later wars in Africa in the 1990s.

Geographical contagion explains cross-border recruitment or deployment of child soldiers. Apart from Stedman's conclusion that conflicts in SSA are contagious,[43] the close territorial proximity between two or more countries or theatres of conflict, loosely policed borders and regimes' disposition towards child soldiering or the availability of sanctuaries to non-state armed groups are important "catalysts" in promoting trans-border child soldiering. The movement of thousands of southern Sudanese children all the way through Kenya, to Ethiopia for military training in the 1980s, is a case in point, as it typifies the geographical contagion phenomenon.

In both Liberia and Sierra Leone, elements of the geographical contagion effects are discernible, even though distinctions can be drawn. Indeed, while precedence was surely at work in Liberia, a combination of geography and precedence is observable in the case of Sierra Leone. The initial 150-man NPFL army could not have been expected to effectively challenge the larger and better armed AFL without expanding recruitment to include children, a decision for which they could draw on the precedents in Angola, Ethiopia, Mozambique, Uganda, and Sudan in the 1980s. In his comparison of the rebellions in Liberia and Sierra Leone, Paul Richards likened the executions carried out by the RUF to the earlier ones in Mozambique by RENAMO.[44] In a similar study Riley also argued that the "style and the horror of war are similar...involve child soldiers, ritual deaths, extensive human rights abuses..."[45]

Precedence contagion in Sierra Leone was augmented by that of geography through the use of child soldiers in neighbouring Liberia where the close logistical and strategic linkages between the NPFL and RUF were enhanced by the geographical propinquity with Liberia. This factor combined with President Taylor's continued support for the RUF/AFRC, and the loosely policed borders between Liberia and Sierra Leone do encourage the emergence of a geographical contagion effect[46] by facilitating cross-country recruitment and deployment of child soldiers. This phenomenon is corroborated by Richards' observation that the area controlled by the RUF was directly connected to NPFL territory by numerous smuggling tracts through the forest, and that young people in the area often belonged to families divided by the border, and that before the war they routinely maintained both Sierra Leonean and Liberian identities.[47]

1.4 Child Soldiers as Threats to Security
The United Nations Security Council (UNSC) resolution 1261 (1999) expressly stated grave concern at "the harmful impact and widespread impact of armed conflict on children and the long-term consequences this has for durable peace, security and development."[48] The Security Council resolution 1314 (2000)[49] not only confirms their security relatedness, but also invites us to situate the phenomenon within the evolving debate in the broader security studies. Security in this context relates to any existential threat(s). It is about the survival of a designated referent object tradition-

ally, but not necessarily, the state. The end of the Cold War has served as a catalyst for challenging the dominant traditional (realist/neorealist) thesis on security, hence the emergence of the critical security studies. The alternative conception of this genre of works represents a bunch of mixed approaches including post-modern realist that seeks to widen the security dragnet beyond the orthodox state-as-unitary actor, politico-military and security dilemma model. They include a wider range of threats ranging from economic and environmental issues to forced migration. The deepening agenda also include the role of individuals and by extension, child soldiers in contemporary security debates.

By situating this study within the core issues in the security debate such as; what and who (referent object) is to be secured, from what threats (securityness), and by what means (securitization), it sides with the critical security school, thus rejecting certain 'core' realist assumptions. It acknowledges the possibility of five levels of analysis thus transcending the state-international structure limitation to include individuals, sub-state units (lobbies and bureaucracies) and subsystem units (regional bodies).[50]

The study, accordingly, challenges the neorealist methodological individualism where all social action is the product of the interaction of rational subjects. States are synonymous with security and serve to guarantee the security of citizens; citizenship then becomes the threshold between security and insecurity. With states-as-unitary actors responding to external threats, anarchy thus becomes a permanent condition of international relations. We posit here that this conclusion results from the *a priori* claims about individual-state relations and a contracted political order embedded in the contractual theory of sovereignty rather than any objective reality.[51] The idealist argument of an externally directed notion of security also falls prey to the present argument, which is anchored in Acharya's submission that experiences in the Third World challenge the realist opinion of the state as the provider of security, for the state has in many ways been a primary source of insecurity. [52]

20

Most prevailing senses of insecurity in the Third World are from within, despite the rhetoric of their elites to the contrary. Where external threats exist, they are mostly due to internal factors (vulnerabilities). Thus, at best, the relationship between internal and external factors is symbiotic.[53] Hence security in the Third World is defined in relation to vulnerabilities that threaten or have the potential to bring down or weaken state structures, both territorially and institutionally, as well as the governing regime. Accordingly, the primary cause of Third World instability is located domestically. It is within this framework that child soldiers become central to the discourse.

Within the critical security studies debate, reaction to the realist charge of intellectual incoherence[54] is to adopt a post-modern realist position of a statist approach and a multi-sectoral focus that incorporates the economic, political, military and social spheres. This multi-sectoralism is especially necessary in analyzing African security given the juridical as opposed to the empirical statehood in SSA. Most states in Africa are inadequately explained by the orthodox-Weberian-monopoly state. The absence of positive sovereignty[55] occasioned first, by the prevalence of poverty—for instance the region's GDP for 1992 ($270)—was appreciably less than that of the Netherlands,[56] over half (340m) of its 600m population lives on less than $1 per day and thirty four of its fifty-three states are among the least developed in the world .[57]

Besides that, shadow state practices and patrimonial politics have further weakened the already fragile national consensus by intensifying divisions along ethnic and regional lines to produce "lame leviathans." [58] Hence, states or governments in the region emerge as instruments of oppression, lose the monopoly of force and become a source of bitter contestations and by implication, the greatest source of insecurity rather than security. Multisectoralism allows for the selection of some distinctive patterns of interaction to reduce complexity and facilitate clarity and analysis. It also maintains interoperability between the old and new approaches, enabling the latter to incorporate smoothly the insights of the former. Thus, in this study the military sector or threat is defined as any relationship of force or coercion, while the economic sector covers threats emanating from relationships of trade, production and finance. The social sector, on the other hand, covers threats to social cohesion, relationships and traditional societal values; while the political sector covers relationships of authority, governing status, recognition and regime stability.[59]

This study departs, then, from the realists' sole emphasis on politico-military issues such as "strategic reductionism" resulting from the militarization of security studies and its policy linkage during the Cold War. It incorporates non-military threats such as security software,[60] in its exploration of threats to referent objects. Accordingly the security software involves legitimacy, integration or societal cohesion and policy capacity.

Consequently, the study adopts Ayoob's securitization criterion which is the ability to effect or influence political outcomes. Using Easton's authoritative allocation of values, then, security is seen as essentially political. All threats are constituted and defined politically, where issues such as economics, child soldiers, etc., threaten either to have political consequences or are perceived to have potentials to threaten the boundaries of states, political institutions or governing regimes, they become part of a state's security dilemmas or calculus.[61] Thus political order is justified by the fact that without it, every other form of security is likely to remain elusive, or at best, ephemeral. Security is located within the political while being sensitive to the other realms or variables that may have impact on political outcomes. The definitional scope of the present work is multifaceted in nature, it retains its analytical utility and avoids pitfalls of undue elasticity by delimiting security. It seeks a re-definition rather than a de-definition of security, and allows us to simultaneously deal with the security hardware (capabilities) as well as the software (interactions).[62] By focusing on the role of domestic factors such as child soldiering, it advocates a bottom-up rather than the realist top-down analysis of national their security.

1.5 Project Objectives

The broad objective of the study was to critically examine the impact of the civil wars in Liberia and Sierra Leone on children as combatants, and the implications for post conflict peace building in those societies in particular, and West Africa in general. The specific objectives were:

i)   To assess the extent to which "child soldiers" were involved in internal conflicts in West Africa, especially in the Sierra Leonean and Liberian civil wars,

ii)   To extensively document the activities of children, especially child soldiers, during the conflict, the tasks assigned to them and their place in the overall scheme of war in the two countries,

iii) To investigate the reasons for children's participation in the civil conflicts in Liberia and Sierra Leone, the process of their recruitment, as well as the legal and political implications,

iv)   To examine the impacts of these factors on the courses and management of the civil wars in Liberia and Sierra Leone,

v)   To examine the impact of the civil wars in the two countries on adolescents by assessing their psychological dispositions focusing on identifying personality disorders and impaired functioning following their long exposure to the traumatic experiences of active combatants, and

vi)   To use the experiences of child combatants in Liberia and Sierra Leone to highlight the implications for post conflict reconstruction and peace building and the need for a regional blueprint for coming to grips with the problem.

1.6 Significance of the Project

The prevalence of armed conflicts in West Africa in the aftermath of the end of the Cold War is gradually nurturing what can be loosely called a martial culture in the sub-region. Thousands of kids and youths have been inducted into a culture of violence not just in Liberia and Sierra Leone but also in countries such as Nigeria and once peaceful Cote d'Ivoire. The

23

most important aspect of this culture of violence is the phenomenon of child soldiers, which attracted attention only during the wars and because of the atrocities committed by child soldiers. Significantly, not much attention has been directed to examining the reintegration of these children into post-conflict societies and the impact that that could have on effective peace building in war-torn societies like those in Liberia and Sierra Leone. Yet the success or failure to effectively de-traumatize and reintegrate child combatants into civil society in the two countries has decisive implications for political and economic development as well as nation building because of its sociological effects. Thus, the phenomenon must be investigated properly and given appropriate attention especially in post war or post conflict reconstruction and peace building efforts. The project is designed to address some of these salient issues, which most existing studies have so far ignored.

1.7 Project Scope
The study covered the period starting with the outbreak of the Liberian civil war in December 1989 to the end of the civil war in Sierra Leone in early 2002, which culminated in presidential and general elections in that country that year. The study departs from previous ones by examining the roles of children in civil wars in Liberia and Sierra Leone and the impacts of the wars on child soldiers focusing on their wartime experiences, post trauma stress disorders in former combatants and the role of multilateral agencies in post conflict reconstruction in the two countries.

1.8 Methodology
Given the mainly qualitative nature of the study, two sources of data were utilized: primary and secondary. For primary sources, in-depth interviews were conducted in the two countries with child soldiers, officials in the national and friendly governments, donor agencies and NGOs responsible for the rehabilitation of child soldiers. Focus Group Discussions, FGDs, were held with segments of civil society in the two countries including students, market women, religious and political leaders to elicit

their views on the role of children in the wars, the impact of the wars on children and the post conflict reconstruction efforts in Liberia and Sierra Leone.

The child soldiers were randomly selected using the following factors: age, ethnicity, sex, educational background/level, socio-economic status of parents prior to the civil war, etc., with the aid of key informants. These sources were complemented with observations carried out by the researchers in the two countries during the fieldwork. For secondary data, the study relied on extensive library and Internet search of books, journal articles and newspapers, magazines and reports by international agencies like the UN and its related organs, ECOWAS, as well as those by the NGO community, donor agencies and friendly governments.

Notes and References

1. See for instance, Sola Akinrinade and Amadu Sesay (1998) (eds.), **Africa in the Post-Cold war International System,** (London: Frances Pinter), and UNRISD (1995), **States of Disarray: The Social Impacts of Globalization,** Geneva: UNRISD.
2. The tribunal has since swung into action and some prominent officials in Tejan Kabba's Government have been arrested for war crimes. The most prominent so far, perhaps, is the former Minister Hinga Norman. Again, on 3rd June 2003, the Tribunal issued a warrant of arrest for the Liberian President, Charles Taylor, for his role in the war in Sierra Leone, while he was in Ghana attending a peace conference called by ECOWAS leaders at Akosombo. At the time of writing the LURD Movement had pushed towards the capital, Monrovia, and there were increasing calls for Taylor to step down. He however refused to do so claiming that stepping down would lead to blood bath, and that the only way to peace was for the Tribunal to drop all the war crimes charges against him after which he would step down as president.

3. Machel, Graca, **The Impact of Armed Conflict on Children**, United Nations: A/510(26 August, 1996). Also at gopher://gopher.un.or:70/00/ga/docs/51/plenary/A51-306.EN

4. See Qtunnu, Olara, Protection **of Children Affected by Armed Conflict- Being the Third Report of the Special Representative of the UN Secretary General for Children and Armed Conflict.** UNGA A/55/442 (3 October, 2000).

5. Otunnu, 3 October 2000.op.cit

6. The equivocation in article 77 of 1977 Additional Protocol 1 on direct/indirect military capacities. The 16 year-old recruitment provision by national armed forces implies that a measure of institutional child soldiering is permissible even though proof of The equivocation in article 77 of 1977 Additional Protocol 1 on direct/indirect participation has been repeated under the 2000 optional protocol to the CRC by only banning the use of children in only active age and parental/volunteer consent is required. Again, our institutional/non-institutional categories help in understanding the legal context.

7. See Stohl, Rachel., 'Africa Reacts to Child Soldiers Problem'. De-fence Monitor, (Washington, D.C.: Centre for Defence Information 29 April 1999. It is Available at www.cdi.org.

8. This percentage is got given the total global estimate of 3000,000 cases and the African figure of 120,000.

9. Wessels, Mike., "Child Soldiers" .Chicago: *Bulletin of the Atomic Scientists,* Nov/Dec (1997), 7.

10. Goodwin-gill, G. & Cohn, I. **Child Soldiers: The Role of Children in Armed Conflict.** (Oxford: University Press, 1994, 62.

11. Ressler, Tortorici & Marcelino. **Children in War: A Guide to the Provision of Services,** A Study for Unicef, New York: UNICEF, 1993, 114

12. Bennet, T.W. **Using Children in Armed Conflict: A Legitimate African Tradition?** Monograph 32, Pretoria: Institute of Strategic Studies, 1999, 4. Also available at www.iss.co.za.

13. Stedman, Stephen. John., " Conflict and Conciliation in Sub-Saharan Africa" in Brown, E. Michael (.ed,) **The International Dimension of Internal Conflict**. London: MIT Press, 1996, 238.
14. SIPRI. **SIPRI Year Book 2000: Armaments, Disarmament and International Security**. (Oxford University Press, Oxford: 2000), 17.
15. For a list of theatres of war involving child soldiers, see Brett, k & McCallin, M. **Children: The Invisible Soldiers**. (Radda Barnen, Stockholm: 2000.), 16-17.
16. Article 21 of the African Charter on the Rights and Welfare of Children emerged as thefirst child's rights law prohibiting the recruitment and use of any person less than eighteen years in a military capacity.
17. For example the Iroghae and Amabutho age sets in Benin and Zulu ethnic groups respectively. See Bennet, op cit. 6-9.
18. For example Shaka the ruler of Zulu Kingdom in Southern Africa drafted under eighteen year-olds into the Aamabutho and Iintanga age sets in the 19th century. See Bennet op cit, .9.
19. Furley, Oliver. 'Child Soldiers in Africa' in Furley, Oliver ed. **Conflict in Africa**. (Tauris, London: 1995.), 6.
20. Bennett op cit, 12.
21. Ibid.
22. Craighton, Alistair., "Shame of the Innocents Forced to Take up Arms". *The Scotman,* (29 July, 2000.), p.7. See also Furley, 1995 op cit, 29.
23. This is a general conclusion of childcare agencies working in Freetown. For instance see Amnesty International, "Sierra Leone: War Crimes Against Children Continue," **Press Release,** (19 June 2000.) , 2 .
24. Goodwin-gill and Cohn coined the phrase to describe the influence of parents, families, peer groups, religion and other community-based institution in a child's subjective evaluation of events and ubsequent decision to enlist. See Goodwin-gill, G. & Cohn, I. **Child Soldiers:**

The Role of Children in Armed Conflict., New York: Oxford University, 1994., 30.

25. Abdullah, Muana & P., I "The Revolutionary United Front of Sierra Leone: A Revolt of the Lumpen Proletariat" in Clapham, Christopher (ed.), **African Guerrillas,** London:James Currey Limited, 1998, 186.

26. Honwana, A. "Negotiating Post-War Identities: Child Soldiers in Mozambique and Angola." **CODESRIA Bulletin** 1&2 1999 (1999), 4-12.

27. The earliest massive use of children as soldiers in Africa is associated with liberation movements in Angola, Mozambique, Southern Sudan, South Africa and Eritrea.

28. Shadow state describes the emergence of rulers drawing authority from their abilities to control markets and their material rewards-deliberate undermining of state institutions for personal gains. See Reno, William. **Corruption and State Politics in Sierra Leone,** (Cambridge: Cambridge University Press, 1995, 3.

29. In the early 1980s, the Mengistu regime in Ethiopia had the largest African army-450, 000 men, including child soldiers. While it tried to contain agigtation for independence by the Eritrean Peoples Liberation Front, it was also suspicious of external subversion having been surrounded by Muslim dominated states. See Bredal, M., 'Disarmament and Demobilization After Civil Wars.' **Adelphi Paper** 303 (International Institute for Strategic Studies. Oxford: Oxford University Press, August 1996, 20.

30. Aboagye, F.B. **ECOMOG:A Sub-Regional Experience in Conflict Resolution, Management and Peacekeeping in Liberia,** Accra: Sedco, 1999, 44

31. Human Rights Watch. **Easy Prey: Child Soldiers in Liberia** (Human Rights Watch, New York: 1994.) and Human Rights Watch, **Sierra Leone: Sowing Terror: Atrocities Against Civilians in**

Sierra Leone, New York: Human Rights Watch, July 1998, Vol. 10, no 3(a)).

32. Human Rights Watch, 1994 op cit, .3.
33. See UNICEF; **Children as Victims,** October 2000, available at www.unicef.org
34. Abdullah and Muana op cit, 186.
35. Kelly, David, **The Disarmament, Demobilization and Reintegration of Child Soldiers in Liberia, 1994-1997: The Process and Lessons Learned,** New York: Unicef 1998, 13.
36. The 'San San boys' is a local name for illegal diamond miners. Potes were centres where children (school drop-outs) and young unemployed converge for recreational drugs and share Lumpen (despair) political views.
37. Goodwin-gill, G. & Cohn, I. **Child Soldiers: The Role of Children in Armed Conflict,** (New York: Oxford University Press, 1994., 30-53.
38. Aboagye op cit, p. 230-232.
39. These were the general weapons used in the two wars. In fact, the Kamajors also used simpler weapons including machetes and knives.
40. Machel Report op cit, para.27.
41. For more discussion on contagion effects see Ismail, O.M "The Role of Child Soldiers in National Security: A Comparative Analysis of Liberia and Sierra Leone", unpublished M.Phil thesis, Center for International Studies, University of Cambridge, 2001 10-21.
42. On the nature of insurgency movements in Africa, see Clapham, Christopher, 'Analyzing African Insurgencies' in Clapham, Christopher (ed.), **African Guerrillas,** (James Currey Limited, United Kingdom: 1998.), 1-18.
43. Stedman, Stephen. John. " Conflict and Conciliation in Sub-Saharan Africa" in Brown, E.M (ed.), **The International Dimension of Internal Conflict,** (MIT Press, London: 1996),.248-49.

44. Richards, Paul. "Rebellion in Liberia and Sierra Leone: A Crisis of Youth?" in Furley, Oliver (ed.), **Conflict in Africa,** (London: Tauris 1995), 139.

45. Riley, Stephen., "Liberia and Sierra Leone: Anarchy or Peace in West Africa?"_Conflict Studies_ 287, London: Research Institute for the Study of Conflict and Terrorism, 1996, 13.

46. The U.N in 2001 confirmed the link between RUF rebellion and cross border activities from Liberia. See BBC News/Africa. *Liberia: Where Rebels Roam Free,* (14 June 2000). Available at http://news.bbc.co.uk/hi/english/world/africa/newsid_788000/788911.stm

47. Richards, P. op cit, 159.

48. See S/RES/1261 (1999) para1, available at www.un.org

49. See S/RES/1314 (2000), para 1, available at www.un.org

50. Buzan, B., Waever, O. and de Wilde, J. **Security: A New Framework for Analysis, London:** Lynne Rienner, 1998, 6.

51. Krause and Williams., *International Studies Review* (1996) 40, p.232.

52. Acharya, Amitav. 'The Periphery as the Core: The Third World and Security Studies' in Krause, K. & Williams, M. C. (eds.) **Critical Security Studies: Concepts and Cases,** London: UCL Press, 1997, .303.

53. Ayoob, Mohammed. 'Defining Security: A Subaltern Realist Perspective' in Krause, K. & Williams, M.C. (eds.) **Critical Security Studies: Concepts and Cases,** London: UCL Press, 1997, 51.

54. Buzan, Waever and de Wilde op cit, 4.

55. This relates to ineffective governance in many states in SSA. Jackson 1986 proposed the term juridical statehood to describe the negative role of governments in SSA and the external nature of legitimacies of many regimes in the region. See Jackson, Robert. : Negative Sovereignty in Sub-Saharan Africa". _Review of International Studies_ 12 (Great Britain, 1986), 254.

56. Clapham, Christopher. **Africa and the International System: The Politics of State Survival**, Cambridge: University Press, 1996,164.
57. B. Krause and Williams, op. cit; *International Studies Review* (1996) 40, 232 and Acharya, Amitav, "The Periphery as the Core: The Third World and Security Studies" in Krause, B and Williams, M.C. (1997)(eds.) **Critical Security Studies, Concepts and Cases**, London: UCL Press, 51. This relates to ineffective governance in many satates in SSA. Jackson (1996), proposed the term juridical statehood to discribe the negative role of governments in SSA and the BBC Africa Presents its Big Idea (22nd July 2001). Available at http://news.bbc.co.uk/hi/english/world/africa/newsid_1448000/1448758.stm
58. Thomas Callaghy uses the phrase to depict the poor institutional capacity building of many African states due to large bureaucracies manned by less skilled civil servants. Callaghy cited in Stedman op cit, 254.
59. Buzan, Waever and de Wilde, op cit, p.7.
60. Azar and Chung Moon cited in Ayoob, op cit. 11.
61. Ayoob, 1996, op cit, 129.
62. Ibid, 129-131.

Section Two: The Nature and Dynamics of Civil Wars in West Africa

Chapter Two: The Nature and Character of Civil Wars in West Africa in the 1990s

Celestine O. Bassey

With the decline of the cold war; regional conflicts will tend to become more local than global, caused by intensifying structural inequalities rather than by incompatible national interests. Global trends towards détente and disarmament increase pressures on African leaders to permit political discourse and facilitate peace process. Yet external as well as internal divergences perpetuate many of the conditions for conflict[1]

2.1 Introduction

The phenomenon of collapsed states in West Africa and its systemic manifestations in civil disorder and humanitarian tragedies of incalculable proportion in Chad, Liberia and Sierra Leone, has been a subject of unabating international concern. These civil conflicts, *"the symptom of collapse* of civil order"*, represent an aggravating trend that is anchored to the "visceral ties of ethnicity and religion that transcend boundaries... compelling governments to seek new forms of activism when civil conflicts occur"[2]. While these accelerating concerns of domestic conflagration are not new in the post-colonial states of West Africa, their outbreak in the 1990s has been characterized by the "absence of legitimate sovereignty manifested in collapsing central governments" and accompanied by the rise of novel warfare strategies, such as "ethnic cleansing, child soldiers, mass rape, banditry, starvation, and the use of mercenaries"[3]. The pervasiveness and intensity of this criminalisation of violent domestic rivalries generally made the resolution or management of such conflicts extremely problematic. As Edward Kolodzeiej and William Zartman have noted:

Such states and warring groups are trapped in what Barry Buzan characterizes as an immature anarchy. The rivals tend to view their security relations as a zero-sum game in which the perceived gain of

35

one side is viewed as a loss for the other. Concessions and compromises are interpreted as signs of weakness, as sellouts, or even as traitorous acts by contesting factions within a group or state in conflict with a common external foe[4].

This chapter seeks to provide a theoretical exploration of this syndrome of domestic conflict vortex, which, in the 1990s provided the context for the brutal manifestation of one of the horrific humanitarian tragedies of our time (the phenomenon of "child soldiers") in Africa. The analysis focuses on the nature and structural dynamics, which "condition the emergence and behaviour of actors",[5] in civil wars in West Africa. In the process, it highlights the changing social and policy context in the sub-region (spanning the Cold and post-Cold War eras), which sustained a vortex of civil disorder as the crisis of regime legitimacy and social fragmentation engulfed some countries in the sub-region. Thus, the taxonomy and analysis of the structural and psycho-cultural conditions, which generate the "manifest conflict processes" in West African social systems, will necessarily center on historical dynamics and precedents, current manifestations and permutations, as well as processes of change. It argued that fundamental continuity and discontinuity exist between the two eras (pre and post 1990s) in terms of the nature and dynamics of civil wars in West Africa bearing on the changing configuration of actors, mode of engagements and outcome.

2.2 The West African Vortex

Civil wars are generally considered large-scale organized domestic violence, which "revolve around processes of political change, and are comprised of state-building conflicts, and major power influence-building conflicts". According to Conteh-Morgan:

> On the one hand, these two types of conflict could, and sometimes did interact directly and/or overlapped. On the other hand, they are structured by the intersection between domestic and external power political objectives. While external powers tried to establish new

36

power political relations, nation-builders were caught between the two rivals, or wanted to steer an independent course[6].

As a sub-region comprising states of recent colonial origin, West Africa has been caught in a vortex of such traumatic social conflict which in a number of cases (Nigeria, Chad, Liberia, Sierra Leone, Guinea Bissau) threatened to destroy the social fabric of the societies involved. Pressures arising from domestic fissures, combined with widespread irredentism, vigilantism and external intervention engendered a spiral of violence with incalculable consequences for the stability and development of these states in particular, and the sub-region in general.

The tremendous diversity presented by ethnic compositions, socio-economic structures, and physical characteristics of the sub-region has had far-reaching spatial consequences for the nature and dynamics of the conflicts and the role of military forces in their resolution. As is readily seen in the "raucous decades" of the 1970s and 1980s, the diffusion of military capabilities and the decentralization of initiative in threatening or using them increased the chances for armed confrontation (e.g. Burkina Faso and Mali) in the sub-region.

While the roots of these conflicts are invariably local, the dynamics (including technologies), which fueled them, were more often than not tied to regional and global rivalries, as, for example, the Nigerian Civil War and the battle for control of Chad. The logic of this linkage (between local, regional, and global forces) resides in a historical and complex interaction between extra-continental interests and regional economic, political, and ideological imperatives, as seen in the hegemonic presence of France in Franco-phone West Africa. The low levels of economic, industrial and structural development in the regions paved the way for the rapid internalization of conflict, "since most of these states have the capacity to initiate a war yet seldom the wherewithal to sustain it." [9] This internationalization of conflict has in the past, resulted in geopolitical rivalry among the dominant powers, which in turn sustains domestic conflagration, as in Nigeria and Chad. Thus, Kolodziej and Zartman have argued succinctly that:

> The globalization of a conflict and its intensification in regional struggles are rooted in several structural sources endemic to the nation-state system. The first is simply a function of the multilateralization of arms production and transfers, including military technology, which sustain, widen, and make regional armed clashes more destructive than ever before... The devastation wrought by a local conflict that heretofore might have been limited by the inability of hostile groups and states to gain access to advanced weapons is now facilitated by the destructive efforts of other states, driven by their own security and welfare interests, to furnish these implements of war to belligerents[7].

Seen in the above context, civil wars in West Africa could be considered a microcosm of a wide range of conflict development in Third World social formations. It could thus be constructed as a dramatic and extreme manifestation of what Sandole has termed "manifest conflict processes" (MC Ps): situations in which at least two actors or their representatives try to "pursue their perceptions of mutually incompatible goals by undermining directly or otherwise, the goal-seeking capability of one another"[8]. Explaining these conflict-developments, therefore, involves a critical appraisal of both the structural conditions and the psycho-cultural factors, which sustain the scale and intractability of conflict vortex in the West African sub-region, especially in the 1990s. The structural conditions direct attention to forces, which "can make a society more or less prone than another to particular levels and forms of conflict and violence." The psycho-cultural dispositions determine the overall level of conflict in a society in terms of shared assumptions, perceptions and images about what "people in a society value, their definitions of friends and foes", and the means which groups and individuals use to promote or defend their goals. In other words, structural analyses of conflict, violence and warfare focus on how the 'organisation of society shapes action, whereas psycho-

38

cultural explanations look to the actors themselves and how they interpret the world"[9].

In the Cold War period, these "manifest conflict processes" developed within the context of global conflict dynamics, which impacted on the African subsystem. That is, the extent to which the basic structure of the international system, the degree to which it is sustained by ideological rivalry, and the relative instability of the states that comprise it set the contextual parameters for Africa's regional rivalries, arms build-ups, political instabilities, civil strife and decolonization process in Africa. It thus became necessary, when examining the dynamics of violence in the domestic formations of West Africa, to (i) explore the relationship between intra-regional and extra-regional (global) interactions; (ii) relate such interactions to attributes of actors; iii) examine the relationship between interactions and conflict patterns; and (iv) develop an issue-based typology of conflict dynamics and responses involving large scale physical violence.

In other words, as several experiences involving the conservative pro-Western francophone 'axis' of Senegal -Cote d'Ivoire - Gabon - Zaire with extra-continental actors in regional crisis demonstrated, the power elite in the sub-region were on the throes of ideological imbroglio. This situation reinforces and sanctions the external presence, which many others on the continent were inclined to consider dysfunctional to African interests. In this context, the regional dynamics and domestic factors, which fuelled prevailing conflict spirals are linked to powerful systemic forces. The unresolved legacy of colonialism combined with ethnic fragmentation, ideological and personality differences among the power elite to engender domestic turbulence, which includes and paves the way for external intervention. As was seen in Chad, the internationalization of domestic conflict gave vent to superpower geostrategic rivalry on the continent. Because of their divergent and competitive orientations, the core powers always invariably supported opposing sides, thereby indirectly transferring their rivalry into local conflicts. And through the "assistance" they render, they make their interests a factor in the genesis as well as the outcomes of such conflicts. In other words, since internal or intra-regional wars may engender profound social change, which is fundamentally unpredictable (and "no situation is more threatening to nations than one whose outcome has become so uncertain as to have moved beyond their control"), it is in the interest of the core powers to ensure favourable results by intervening.

However, in the post-Cold War permutation in security system relations among the core powers, the pattern of conflict development in the sub-region has become more internalized and complex in terms of actors, issues, and outcome, as the turbulence of democratization, mass concretization, crisis of legitimacy, stagflation, anomie, uneven development, mounting external debt, ethno-linguistic fractionalization and religions fundamentalism unleash devastating social conflict in a number of these countries. As is generally reflected in the literature, the post-Cold War development wrought by "Gorbachev's revolution" had significant implications for conflict processes in the sub-region as it brought about a dramatic shift in the "threat perceptions" of dominant powers whose defence and foreign policy concerns were " so firmly interlinked with those of the international system as to make them virtually indistinguishable" .[10]

By initiating major policy alteration in Russian military diplomacy (the use of Russian armed forces as an instrument of policy), the Post-soviet administration in Russia has virtually altered the paradigm of superpower strategic relations as the era of confrontation and adverse partnership *prima facie* gives way to accommodation and coexistence. Consequently, the post Cold War Russian-American détente has affected the global structure of conflict interaction and escalation through intervention. The implications of this altered context of international strategic relations have been profound and dramatic in terms of possibilities for conflict resolution in the African regional system. This emerging condition derived from what is now seen as the principle of "correct reciprocity" in US-Russian relations:

each power consciously desists from actions that may be interpreted as an attempt to create an exclusive sphere of influence or "impinge upon the traditional geo-political interests of the opposite side" [11].

Thus, as one analyst noted, an "important challenge facing the great powers and the Third World countries in the settlement of regional conflicts is to minimize their involvement while maximizing their contribution to the search for political solutions" [12]. As a consequence, the character and terrain of civil conflicts and wars in the West African sub-region in the post-Cold War era became more macabre (with rebel excesses in Sierra Leone and Liberia), more localized in terms of protagonists and *causus belli* and more devastating in terms of societal impacts. They are wrenched by crises of domestic political consensus that involved an "extra-ordinary complex mix of factors including multi-ethnic and communal cleavages and disintegrations, underdevelopment and poverty and distributive justice"[13]. In this regard, Earl Conteh-Morgan has trenchantly noted that:

> African internal conflicts had been affected by a long period of US-Soviet rivalry and now a post-cold war era and virtual military disengagement in the continent. Three decades after independence, Africa, like many other regions of the world, is undergoing a deep transformation, which is manifested in new scenarios in conflict and militarization[14].

In Earl Conteh-Morgan's appraisal, " four unfolding scenarios" could presently be observed which "impact, either directly or indirectly, on the scope, intensity, or duration of conflict in the continent". These novel conflict manifestations are: "conflicts generated by the democratization drive sweeping across the continents; conflicts related to Structural Adjustment Programs (SAP); regional and/or external interventions on humanitarian grounds; and the emergence of regional hegemony (very influential regional powers) and their impact on the outcome of conflicts and militarization." Thus, judging from the extreme variegated character of internal convulsion in the West African sub-region (from the communal mayhem in Nigeria to civil disturbances in Cote d'Ivoire, a failed putsch in Bissau and carnage in Sierra Leone and Liberia), one would readily agree with Mary Kaldor, that a

> "new type of organized violence has emerged since the 1980s and the early 1990s, characterized by a blurring of the lines between war, organized crime, and large-scale human rights violations; these conflicts demonstrate new modalities of conflict goals and the means of warfare; which distinguish them from earlier civil-wars." [15]

This Hobbessian nightmare has been given extreme articulation by Kaplan in his extensively cited piece, "The Coming Anarchy".

> West Africa is becoming the symbol of worldwide demographic, environmental, and societal stress, in which criminal anarchy-emerges as the real 'strategic' danger. Disease, overpopulation, unprovoked crime, scarcity of resources, refugee migrations, the empowerment of nation-states and international borders, and the empowerment of private armies, security firms, and international drug cartels are most tellingly demonstrated through a West African prism. West Africa provides an appropriate introduction to the issues, often extremely unpleasant to discuss, that will soon-confront our civilization [16]

Kaplan's observation underscores the variety of characterization of 'civil wars' in West Africa in the post-Cold War era by an array of commentators: 'post-modern wars'[17]; 'intra-state wars', 'small wars' or 'limited wars'[18]; ethnic wars' or 'ethnic conflicts'[19], and more generally, "security predicament"[20]. However, despite these characterizations, empirical indicators reinforce Richard Jackson's position that there is "sufficient continuity in the nature, forms, and goals of the conflicts to incorporate traditional forms of civil war, as well as more recent phenomena like failed states, warlord politics, genocide, the use of mercenaries and private security firms, and general civil violence"[21]. In others, considered from the standpoint of actors, issues, strategies and outcomes of current civil conflicts and wars in West Africa, there are fundamental continuity and discontinuity from past traditional forms of irredentism, vigilantism and wars of secession and hegemonic control by contending social forces (e.g. Nigeria and Chad). On this view:

> The nature of internal conflict, therefore, demonstrates significant continuities from both periods. It is essentially the same kind of conflict, even through internal and external changes to states and the system mean enhanced opportunities for more extreme forms of violence. What we are witnessing is not some entirely new form of conflict, but rather adaptations in a type of conflict that is historically rooted in the structures and processes of weak states[22]

Nevertheless, the growing complexity of transnational relations engendered by the processes of globalisation have definitely broadened the scope, goal and type of actors, criminalized conflict arena, and mode of exchange, and made the outcome of the ferocious struggles more uncertain. Thus, in Sierra Leone, Liberia, and Chad, the battle space was dominated not only by the opposing forces of government and the rebels, but also by a spectrum of bounty hunters, and other contending actors: "organized militias, warlords, criminal gangs, drug cartels and indigenous NGOs, mercenaries, entrepreneurs and international capitalists". Equally, the engagements also "demonstrated an expanded repertoire of strategies for pursuing conflict goals which describe the horrors experienced by civilian population": ethnic cleansing, mass rape, genocide, policide, mutilation, starvation, and child soldiers"[23], and the outcome has been equally convulsive: settling into "almost permanent conditions of state collapse in Chad, warlordism in Liberia and cycles of "cease-fire followed by further outbreaks of fighting in Sierra Leone". And finally, others have noted that: "The civil war in Sierra Leone has been marked by horrific violence, large-scale torture of civilians, pillage of rural institutions and industrial assets, and mass looting of village property."[24]

The Sierra Leonean experience has raised in poignant form the problem of lumpen culture and political violence that turned teenagers into psychopathic killers. This sociological phenomenon of lumpen youth culture is central to the analysis and comprehension of the core issue of this project-"Child soldiers". This engaging issue - which constitutes the central theme in Wole Soyinka's <u>Open Sore of a Continent</u> - became the major focus of debate by a group of Sierra Leonean scholars on the behavioural propensities of the Revolutionary United Front (RUF) and the Civil War in their country. The challenge here was to address, first, the phenomenon of "street children in an essentially gemeinshcaft environment - the breakdown of social practices such as Mehn Pikin (ward- ship), and the very structure of the extended family structure."

The second epistemic issue is to examine "changes in the incentive structure, which the war may have brought about." As one of the contributors put it:

> The pre-war structure of incentives does not adequately reward marginality, whereas war turns the scales and rewards those who are bold enough to fight... War came to be regarded as a survival strategy by youth who had suffered high levels of social exclusion. Thus, the participation of this category of youth on both rides of the war may partly explain why large-scale atrocities were also committed by the military. The debate highlighted the ways in which the institutions that had previously held lumpen groups in check broke-down and encouraged such groups to cease negotiating for, or demanding, inclusion in the social mainstream, and to opt instead for full-scale brutal violence[25].

A third issue concerned the transformative effect of arms on "estranged youth". This syndrome has been most incisively articulated by Alunda Honwana: the assumption of active combat roles by children in which they become "killer and commit the most horrific atrocities is intrinsically linked

44

to the breakdown of society's structures and morality in the context of the crisis of the post-colonial state"[26]. Under the influence of hallucinogenic drugs and violent psychological pressures "to make them lose their previous identity to assume a new one, they seem to "have committed the most cruel atrocities"[27]. Their socialization process (as was the case with RUF and NPLF) was equally gruesome, as Vine graphically observed:

> Soldiers, some as young as 10 seem to have been put through psychological trauma and deprivation, such as being hung upside down from trees until their individualism is broken, and encouraged and rewarded for killing... these child combatants, who have been programmed to feel little fear or revulsion for such actions, and thereby carry out these attacks with greater enthusiasm and brutality than adults would[28].

On this score analysts have found similarities in values, organization and levels of accountability between RENAMO's violence in Mozambique and that of the RUF in Sierra Leone and NPLF in Liberia. From a comparative perspective, the three movements "were said to be different from classical liberation or decolonization movements and other contemporary armed groups in the continent"[29]. As products of 'lumpen' culture and "resistance to the greed of Africa's post-independence rulers," this category of rebel groups have been motivated less by ideological considerations and more by material considerations in their gladiatorial contest for power. As one contributor observed in his contribution, the "san-san boys" have fought on both sides in the war, and are interested in the violence mainly for self-enrichment. This is in line with what has been observed in the literature about the political behaviour of marginal groups. Marginals are hardly driven by ideology or political principles: they behave instead opportunistically. It would be interesting to study how the RUF's populist message of revolutionary change was expropriated and internalized by the "san-san boys", "rarry mandem" and "njiahugbia gorngeisia". [30.]

45

2.3 Taxonomy of Conflicts

As reflected in the discourse above, civil disorder in West Africa has been multiple and varied and this also provided different circumstances for extensive manifestation of humanitarian catastrophes including the induction of children into combat roles in civil wars. General classifications and typologies of prevailing conflict mode and structural dynamics have been provided in the literature. A broad classification based on the "construction of domestic disorder consolidated variables" has been provided by John Collins (1973), as a framework for analyzing and comprehending civil disorder in West Africa. Collins' construct encompasses composite variables relating to:

i)   Anomic Outbreaks: riots, strikes, political clashes inter-tribal conflict and anti-government demonstrations and mutiny, which constitute general predictors of a breakdown of civil order (as was the case currently in Cote d'Ivoire). As a composite variable, they are similar to Rummel's [31] "turmoil" dimension - a type of domestic disorder that "dictates from national solidarity or is indicative of low domestic solidarity".

ii)   Subversive Activities, which comprise guerrilla warfare, terrorist acts, assassinations and plots. They are generally covert acts of violence directed at achieving fundamental change in the political order. As could be seen in the Mano River Union theatre, subversive activities involve the "actions of counter-elites who are seeking not only to make their dissent known, but also to substitute themselves for the incumbent elites". Again, this composite variable parallels the "subversive" measures of conflict behaviour by Rummel and the "conspiracy dimension" of Ted Gurr[32].

iii) Revolutionary activities, which include political boycotts, anti-government riots, revolutions, and civil wars. According to Collins, this composite variable differs from the first two because they are usually very violent.

46

The fourth, elite instability, and the fifth domestic suppression composite variables, are more indicative of domestic instability, domestic frustrations, domestic tensions, domestic mal-integration, and domestic tension than overt civil war.

Elite instability measures major governmental crisis and usually connotes strong divergent views within the ruling cabal, council or regime. The domestic suppression variable, on the other hand, comprises bans on demonstrations, bans on political groups, proclamation of emergencies or martial law, and freedom of the press curtailments. It can be "conceived to be either an indication of the degree of internal disorder, or the degree of insecurity as perceived and responded to by the governmental elites arising form domestic disorders".[33]

Nevertheless, a combination of these multivariate factors (including "body count" variable - domestic violent deaths) has been widely used as a basis for determining civil war, especially as codified in the ICPSR study. Thus, in a recent contribution to Economic Commission Africa Policy Issue on Conflict, Ibrahim Elbadawi and Nicholas Sambanis combined indicators from several data sets to operationalise the concept of civil war:

> A civil war is an armed conflict that has (I) caused more than 1000 deaths (ii) challenged the sovereignty of an internationally recognized state; (iii) occurred within the recognized boundaries of that state (iv) involved the state as one of the principal combatants; (v) included rebels with the ability to mount an organized opposite, and (vi) involved parties concerned with the prospect of living together in the same political unit after the end of the war[34].

On the basis of these multiple indicators, Donald Morrison and Hugh Stevenson (1971) have, for instance, proffered a mode of conceptualization and typology based on actor categorization: elite, communal groups and mass movements. Subsequent studies of conflict in the African region have tended to utilize this mode of analysis. Lewis Snyder in his study of political disintegration in Third World countries concludes that:

More germane to the security concerns of multi-ethnic developing states is the estimated potential for separatism. The evidence reviewed so far suggests that potential for separatist activity is greatest in developing societies where ethnic cleavages are already deep and where political discrimination against peripheral communities is widely practiced[35].

In Africa, a graphic feature of this phenomenon or "map" is the "extreme vacillation from one block of ethnic support to another with the change of rulers and their regime. In this process, we find the ground of articulation between "class and ethnicity". In Nigeria, Chad, Liberia, Sierra Leone, where "catastrophic balance required between ethnic forces shapes the structures of politics", the "substantial violence required to suppress an ethnic revolt leads to the phenomenon of violence trap where identity and violence reinforce each other. In these instances, conflicts become protracted"[36]. Thus, James Scaritt has argued that:

> The prevalence of communal contenders in black Africa in combination with the existence of other types of minorities raises the questions of the distinctive nature of ethnicity in this region and its relation to other social forces, especially class. In the literature on ethnicity and ethno-political conflict in Africa and around the globe thee is a long-standing debate between primordialists and situationalists[37].

Scaritt's primordialist - situationalist divide in the conceptualization of the structural dynamics of social formations with fundamental cleavages reproduces the "pluralist" - "functionalists" dichotomy and debate represented by the works of M.G. Smith and Emile Durkheim. Often in such societies, however, the prevalent problem of differential incorporation has generally elicited structural conflict resulting at times in revolutionary change.

The functionalist analysis of segmented social order incorporates two processes central to Durkheim's formulation. The first is the process of "individualization" which is manifested in three related forms: social structure, culture and political perception. The second central process evident in Durkheim's analysis is that of group confrontation and accommodation, "in which there is initially "an increasing reliance on the collective organization of ethnically - defined groups, a heightened awareness of ethnic identity, and a more intense hostility". Thus, Durkheim's analysis and projection offer a theoretical basis from the expectation of evolutionary change towards ethnic integration and peace in situations of extreme communal disharmony such as existed in Sierra Leone and Liberia in so far as it involves a conception of increasing contact, harmonious inter-relationship and progressive withering away of ethnic inequality by a process of evolutionary change. The functionalist - cum - situationalist paradigm, thus, visualizes ethnicity:

As an almost totally flexible set of identities that (a) varies from situation to situation depending on rational calculations of advantage, primarily material and political and (b) is stimulated by political mobilization under the leadership of actors whose primary identities and motives are non-ethnic .[38]

While there have been significant moves towards integration in West African Social Systems among divergent ethnic communities over the past century[39], it is now fairly obvious that the "salad" model is more realistic than the "melting pot" model, as a theoretical basis for conflict settlement. In other words, the entrenchment of pristine and cultural boundaries (despite decades of inter -marriages and functional exchanges) still dominates inter-ethnic relationships in most social formations. The expectations arising from the "melting pot" were based on an assumption that in plural societies the individuals, in certain of their roles, will become detached from the original matrix and enter into new relationships across the ethnic lines, thereby creating new inter-ethnic social structures, both formal and informal. Second, in terms of culture, there is an expectation of irreversible process by which individuals come to share many of the same basic institutions as well as a common language. And third, in terms of politics, individuals may take a form in which members of the subordinate

49

group are incorporated progressively into the political system of the dominant group. Sociological support for such development in countries in West Africa since independence is minimal.

The trend is rather graphically represented in the "salad model" which takes the plural conditions in those social formations as given. Instead of fundamental withering away of primordial structures and values the model assumes that new relationships resulting from the progressive division of labour over time are largely superimposed on the old divisions, thereby elaborating rather than changing the plural structure of the society. This trend is supremely evident in the dynamics of conflict in Sierra Leone, Liberia, Nigeria and Chad, among others. In this regard, James Scaritt has concluded that:

> African examples of more intense and violent ethno-political conflict along relatively stable and primordial lines usually involve ethno-nationalist groups, ethno classes, and militant sects; some are long term and others are short-term. On the other hand, conflicts that involve smaller scale but are along even more fixed, primordial lines tend to occur between indigenous peoples who are excluded from governing multi ethnic coalitions or who only wish to be left alone[40]

Although this mode of analysis has provided significant insight to the understanding of the generative structure of domestic fragmentation and conflict in African States, it has been widely seen to be insensitive "either to substantial differences in the form, intensity, and potential effects of conflict episodes that focus on limited issues in contrast with conflicts in which the structure of authority or the integrity of the state is at issue". Thus, Gurr has contended that:

> The distinction between "communal" and "mass" instability is problematique because it implies a sharp division that is often contradicted by African realities. How should we categorize a violent strike by a political association of Zulu Labourers in multi-ethnic South

African township? Are they acting on the basis of communal identities, class position, or membership in a political movement?[41]

Indeed, as historians have generally noted, African towns in the colonial and contemporary context generate "both a social life of their own, unlike any that had previously existed in Africa", and a spirit of African radicalism which transcends primordial and ideological cleavages. In this regard, Geoffrey Barraclough has observed that the exploding population in African towns "threw up a new stratum of tough, emancipated, politically active men, ready to follow bold leadership which knew where it was going." Secondly, they "acted as new focuses of national unity, which cut through tribal divisions and formed urban network binding together Africa's scattered rural communities".[42]

Seen in this context of changing social condition, a simplistic categorization of conflict clusters based on primordial or ideological factors can be patently misleading. On this view, Gurr has provided alternative classification and complex typology of African conflicts involving "'mobilization of people based on several overlapping identities," ethnicity and class and political association, ethnicity and political association - sometimes all three:

Table 2: 1: The Central Issue of Conflict

Primary basis group mobilisation	Policies and Distributional Issues	Position and structures of authority	Intergrity of state
Occupational and class interest Political associations	Strikes, Boycotts Economic Sabotage Political riots, demonstrations	Peasant rebellions Urban uprisings Political revolts revolutionary movements	Regional civil wars
Communal (ethnic) identification	Communal riot, clashes	Communal warfare Genocide	Irredentist/ Autonomist rebellions
Institutional position	Coups Purges	Revolutions from above	
		State terror	
Mutinies		Politicides	

Source: Ted Gurr, "Theories of Political Violence and Revolution in the Third World" in F. Deng and W. Zartman (eds.) **Conflict Resolution in Africa,** (Washington: Brookings Institution, 1991).

51

According to Gurr, in mobilization terms, political association is often the key element underlying these conflict clusters in African social systems:

Demonstration by workers, riots by ethnic minorities, and secessionist movements typically follow from mobilization by leaders who make selective political appeals to communal and class groups and use the organizational tactics of modern political movements. Riots and programs against immigrant workers are another, increasingly common type of conflict that defies simple categorization. The victims are distinguished by, and targeted because of their economic, ethnic, and national status.[43]

Gurr's taxonomy essentially derives from and conflates both instrumentalist and constructivist approaches to the study of ethnicity and ethnic conflict in African social formations. As reflected in Rothchild's[44] analysis, both perspectives provide the theoretical basis for understanding the phenomenon of group cohesion and disintegration that affects oppositional forces in countries such as Sierra Leone, Liberia and Chad, thus creating conditions of domestic quagmire that have generally made conflict settlement an exceedingly difficult task. In Chad, for instance, the civil disorder which surfaced in the mid-sixties as a revolt of the Muslim North against the Southern Christian-dominated central government of Ngarta Tombalaye, had by the late 1970's stalemated into a fearsome contest for power between the two dominant wings of FROLINAT (Front for the Liberation of Chad): FAN and FAP. Allied to these two opposing factions (in a shifting pattern of alignment and realignment) were other splinter groups, which have so far grossly complicated and confounded any hope of a coherent and comprehensive peace plan for Chad. These maverick groups include Movement Pour La Liberation du Tchad (MPLT) led by Abubakar Abdurahaman. Others were the Algiers-based wing of FROLINAT led by Abba Saddigi, the Peoples Liberation Army led by Mohammed Abba and the FROLINAT 'Vulcan Force' led Acyl Ahmat.

It was in the context of this domestic imbroglio, that the OAU undertook its forlorn intervention in 1981[45].

Similarly, what developed from late 1989 as an insurgent revolt by Charles Taylor against the mal-administration of Samuel Doe, had by the mid-1990s degenerated into a fratricidal contest between the remnants of Doe's troops and the two wings of the rebel forces: Taylor's NPFL (National Patriotic Front of Liberia) and Johnson's INPFL (Independent National Patriotic Front of Liberia). Doe's demise and the liquidation of the remnants of his Krahn-dominated government army only set the stage for further proliferation of armed factions (ULIMO-K and ULIMO-J) and the stultification of the peace support operations of ECOMOG. In Sierra Leone, the raging war fought by the State against the rebel forces of the Revolutionary United Front also reflected deep social and ethnic fissures in the Sierra Leonean society. Thus, as observed in the literature, while the 'njiahugbia ngorngeisia' provided the backbone of the RUF combatants, and the 'Kamajoisia militia' fought for the Tejan Kabbah government, the 'rarray boys' and 'san-san boys' fought on both sides of the civil war (on the RUF side and that of Sierra Leone military/kamajor).[46] As one contributor to the debate noted, these 'lumpenmilitariat' were rewarded by the RUF with appointments as 'town commanders' (administrators and militia commanders) in RUF territory and widely considered responsible for most of the "local vendettas, the burning of houses, the tying up and beating of civilians" (halaka and tabay), the identification and killing of some of their own chiefs, Imams and village elders.

In overall terms, variants of topologies of civil disorder have appeared in sociological literature on conflict and conflict behaviour. R. J. Rummel has summarized this literature in his inquiry into the dimensions of conflict behaviour within and between nations[47]. Similarly, Samuel Huntington in his **Political Order in Changing Societies** provided an incisive analysis of conflict" spectrum arising from the general politicization of social forces and institutions." The range of civil disorders often manifested in modernizing societies (strikes, coups, mutinies, revolution, insurgency etc.), are symptomatic of fundamental contradictions in such social systems, according to Huntington. "In such societies, politics lacks autonomy, complexity, coherence, and adaptability"[48]

2.4 Causality

The widespread condition of latent and manifest civil disorder in West Africa over the last couple of decades has generated extensive debate in the literature on the structural and anomic factors sustaining the quasi state of anarchy in these countries. Thus, given its highly indeterminate nature, a spate of literature has developed over the past four decades exploring both the domestic and systemic dimensions of the generative factors sustaining the exploding syndrome of civil war: issues of identity, nationalism, social structure, nation-building and an anarchic and virulently hostile international environment[49]. As could be seen in the literature, investigations and analyses of causes of civil wars in the African continent in general, and in the West African sub-region in particular, in the post Cold War era, have been characterized by profound epistemological divergences[50]. In paradigmatic terms, these literatures have fallen essentially into two major categories. The first, conventional genre, is mechanistic and state-centric, and in analysis and interpretation a "consequence of its micro-orientation, its compartmentalized view of society, its rationalist orientation, and its focus on problems delimited by disciplinary boundaries"[51]. The second, and increasingly more popular radical genre, tends to be dialectical, holistic and system-level in orientation: it construes civil disorder as a resultant of a double antinomy of class and function bearing on Africa's positions in the international division of labour.

Although the literature in the first category is extensive and varied, it focuses in general terms on the dynamics of African social systems. Phenomenal social and economic changes in post-colonial Africa, it has been suggested, manifestly complicate the problem of establishing "new bases of political association and new political institutions combining legitimacy and effectiveness"[52]. This is arguably the consequence of the diversification and multiplication of social forces and the concomitant diminution of traditional sources of political authority, broadening political consciousness, rising expectations and participation. Since, in such a context, as comparative experiences of other regions attest, the rate of social mobilization and the expansion and intensification of political activism outstrip political instability and disorder.

Accordingly, some analysts have sought to expose the objective bases of social systems that have experienced "displacement of roles between adults and children: in which children become killers and commit the most horrific atrocities", such as the crisis of the post-colonial state in Africa. Such crisis in W. Reno's disquisition is "reflected in the ethnic conflicts over power sharing, identity and access to resources; in the incapacity of the state to provide for and protect its citizens; in the collapse of social and economic structures in rural areas and the massive migration to town".[53] Thus in sociological terms, the pervasiveness of armed conflict and violence in which "youth and children are drawn" is symptomatic of such crisis. This view of the generative dynamics of civil war is expressed by a number of historians, anthropologists, and sociologists who sought to explain this manifestation of domestic anarchy as a social and cultural phenomenon[54]. Such a perspective now constitutes the core explanatory variable of civil wars in the plethora of post-Cold War literature that "uses neo-realism in an attempt to make internal war understandable".[55]

A broad spectrum of social scientists have no doubt dismissed neo-realism outright for "ignoring the subtleties of the societies they study, that is, such key factors as identity and social structure". However, a recent spate of contributions to the debate utilizing variants of neorealist conceptual apparatus has sought to address issues of identity and social structures.[56] Utilizing the random effects probit model of the probability of an incident of civil war, Elbadawi and Sambanis came to the conclusion that the fundamental cause of civil war in Africa "is not due to extreme ethno-linguistic fragmentation, but rather to high levels of poverty, heavy dependence on resource-based primary exports and, especially, to failed political institutions".[57] As they both explained:

> While more study is needed to fully understand the socio-economic impact of ethnicity, the macroeconomic strand of this literature has until now not taken fully into consideration the mediating role of political institutions. It is important to understand that ethnic antagonisms take place within the framework of political institutions and that these institutions have the capacity to prevent the escalation of ethnic conflict to the level of violence[58]

Hence, in terms of prognosis for stability in the West African sub-region, they contend that their empirical analysis "leads us to argue that the strategy to prevent civil wars in Africa should be based on promoting political freedom and molding a governance framework that can accommodate Africa's social diversity"[59]. This conclusion provides further supportive evidence and advances the analytical projections of a premier article on "Interactive Model for State-Ethnic Relations."[60]. According to Rothchild, in social systems dominated by deep primordial segmentation, the corresponding regimes (hegemonic exchange and polyarchy) could either engender stable and enduring polity (as in Botswana) or generate latent and manifest period of protracted social conflict (as in Sierra Leone, Liberia, Nigeria, Mali and Togo).

Thus, while "hegemonic regimes" (e.g. Abacha's regime in Nigeria and Doe's of Liberia) that centralized political power and emphasize hierarchical control by government often tend to impose serious constraints on the aggregation and "channeling of group demands to decision elites", "hegemonic exchange" and "polyarchical" regimes allow access to "ethnic intermediaries and are more prepared to enter into direct or tacit negotiations with these interest group intermediaries". [61] The consequences for social system stability, peace and security in both types of state system have been graphically visible in Africa since the 1960s:

> In the hegemonic exchange and polyarchical regimes, leaders fully aware of the fragility of their institutions, are more inclined to enter into ongoing negotiation with a wide array of interest groups in order to promote their state-building objective...yet the tendency on the part of hegemonic regime is to exert central control and to repress social conflicts. The hegemonic regime, a resister of collective demands, thus, tends to repress opposition, inhibit free expression, limit the arena of decision-making, restrict public accountability and, with the exception of the highly ideological states, allow only narrow and restricts opportunities for mass participation. [62]

From both historical and comparative experiences, by suppressing communal and social forces' demands, the hegemonic regimes all too often (Ethiopia, Somalia, Zaire, Sudan etc.) allow festering grievances to explode into open rebellion with incalculable consequences for the society. This situation is usually aggravated by tendency toward military solutions to the ethnic and regional challenges (e.g. the Niger Delta in Nigeria) leading to "intractable conflicts between determined adversaries", as in the Democratic Republic of Congo, DRC, Sierra Leone, Burundi and Rwanda. Hence, the prevailing state of insecurity: "catastrophic balance between ethnic forces shapes the structures of politics", the "substantial violence required to suppress an ethnic revolt leads to the phenomenon of violence trap where identity and violence reinforce each other. In these instances conflicts become protracted". [63]

The extreme manifestations of this travail of political power and its attendant excesses have been the violent collapse of civil order and the emergence of a malignant social condition of insecurity breeding disorder, and repression as "those ruling the state have sought to maintain and preserve their absolute monopoly of power".[64] The irrepressible challenge to this monopoly of state power by the dominant fraction of African elites has been the leitmotiv of the democratic revolt and movement seeking to end decades of despotic rule.

By contrast, the hegemonic exchange and polyarchical regimes (Botswana, Mauritius and Gambia before the current dispensation) by allowing a broader range of representation for competing social forces and responsive channels for the articulation of collective demands, diffuse to a considerable extent latent grievances through the proclivity of a "leader's preparedness to co-opt and engage in limited exchange relations with his country's powerful ethno-regional intermediaries". Systemic stability resulting from this channelisation of latent grievances and a degree of public accountability has generally created a conducive and enabling environment for development in those countries. This is so because:

> More than the hegemonic regime, then, the Polyarchic and hegemonic exchange regimes are processors rather than makers of demands. They are more inclined to accept the legitimacy of autonomous social interests, and in an effort to promote certainty on the part of various national unity [moves] by reconciling and negotiating with these powerful social forces. In large part, their pragmatism is born out of recognition of the "Softness" of their state institutions, yet in some case (Botswana, Senegal), it also demonstrates elite preferences for regulating conflict through more cooperative rituals of encounter.[65]

These manifest regime patterns on the African continent explain the fundamental variation in the genesis and intensity of civil disorder in various African countries: from genocide in Rwanda to ethnic cleansing in Liberia and mayhem in Sierra Leone and Chad. In this regard, the problems posed by neopatrimonial regimes and political transitions in Africa threaten the stability of many countries in the region, given the pervasive use of politics of exclusion even under so called democratic regimes like those in Zimbabwe and Nigeria.

Despite the undeniable insight provided by the above conventional state-centric cluster of literature on the causes of civil war in African social formations, they have been generally found to lack historical contextualisation"[66]. As Duffield summarizes:

> Internal conflicts are more often portrayed in a distinctly positivist light as aberrant forms of political behaviour ...as the breakdown in particular system, or a retreat from normally peaceful political forms and interactions. Emphasising the existence or re-emergence of 'ancient hatreds' or a 'primitive instinct for violence', there is also a stress on element of irrationality, as if persisting civil war ' is a perversion of reason that would otherwise lead men and women to adopt peaceful behaviour'. Both assumptions about the nature of internal conflict - as systemic failure and as defying rational explanation - ignore the considerable objective (and subjective) rationality of employing political violence in politically fragile, circumstances, violence can perform a variety of functions in alternative systems of profit, power and production.[67]

This genre of literature shares one basic, if fallacious, assumption: that civil war in Africa is a preeminent resultant of endogenous or domestic, system-determined variables. This "metaphysical construction of security as stasis and spatial exclusion" entrenches a benign neorealist assumption of the immutability of African social order. A genealogical deconstruction of these rationalistic pretensions in the dominant epistemology on security in Africa calls for, on the one hand, a demystification of latent assumptions and "thought forces" it enshrines. On the other hand, it requires a policy response, which takes account of the changing character and structural deformities of the neocolonial state as the fundamental sources of civil disorder in Africa.

In other words since civil conflict in contemporary international system is very rarely endogenous, the "context of change (exogenous properties) has somehow to be incorporated into the model itself". On this view, a composite theory of instability and violence in countries such as Sierra Leone, Liberia, Nigeria, Mali and Chad, should be anchored not only on the internal dynamics of its social order, but also, "on how that society is inserted into the world system at a particular point in the development of that system".[68] Roxborough explains why:

> The everyday notion that the units of analysis are nation-states or national societies needs to be considered critically. For the societies of the Third World, are by no means well-integrated and homogenous entities... The second consideration is the complement of the first. Just as these societies are badly articulated internally, some parts of them are closely integrated with the metropolis of advanced capitalism[69]

This dialectical and system-centric orientation (internal-disarticulation external-articulation syndrome, as it affects the internal processes of social change, constitutes the "Core-complex" of the radical literature on civil conflagrations in African social formations. The thrust of the argument is necessarily that understanding internal conflicts and wars in peripheral social formations requires a " social theory, or at least a frame of reference based on systematic general categories, in which the historical-developmental aspect is reconstructed with respect to different epochs and which takes into account the structural dynamics which condition the emergence and behaviour of actors". [70] Thus, Mujaju has argued, for instance, that because peripheral formations are "internally incoherent and because aspects of their internal form are projections of the external environment, they are easily manipulated from the outside"[71]. These structural features have been the subject of extensive debate in the literature on "underdeveloped states", "weak states", "quasi-states", "shadow states" or overdeveloped states.[72]

The structural deformities of these peripheral formations manifest in different ways: crisis of legitimacy, political instability, institutional weakness, and lack of national identity, economic scarcity, and external vulnerability. In Africa, these deformities are anchored primarily to the "domestic class structures, production relations and forms of exploitation that sustain neo-colonialism, and the nature of the client post-colonial states that these class structures have developed" also operate to intensify this condition. The destabilizing consequence of these multiple contradictions is, as a number of analysts have noted, been the prevalence of gladiatorial or "exclusionary politics".[73]

Thus, peripheral social formations by this consideration embody the anomaly of existence: state decay. The peripheral feature of this decay in the West African social formations has been the "state's declining capacity to rule or to maintain the conditions for the operation of its eroding productive infrastructures. Three areas of the decline are highlighted by S. W. Sangpam's review article. These are: (i) the "increasing inability of the state to relate national means to policy ends, as seen in the inefficiency of public administration, security forces, economic policies, and so forth, (ii) the decline in probity, manifest in the systemization of corruption[74]. The general response of social forces to this incapacitation of the state has been "withdrawal into survival activities" (e.g. ethnic militias in Nigeria) in one respect, and, in other circumstances (Sierra Leone, Liberia and Chad), the contestation of state power, which often results in a 'zero-sum ethnic struggle for dominance, which may be expressed in violent internal conflict'.[75]. Thus, the forms of withdrawal and "shrinkage of the political arenas" vary from one formation to the other depending on the nature of the conjunctural crisis (to use Gramsci's phraseology): "self-enclosure", "suffer-manage", parallel systems (black markets), guerilla warfare, secessions, regional irredentism, vigilantism, coups, popular revolt (Cote d'Ivoire) and Civil War.[76].

2.5 Synthesis

In terms of its generative structure, the pervasive conflict in West African social systems often displays its own "peculiarities, which must be ig-

61

nored" and in this sense "concrete analyses remain irreplaceable". In this regard, the rapid and relatively extreme breakdown in the structure of the social systems of a number of West African states associated with domestic insecurity results directly from an extraordinary complex mix of factors including "multi-ethnic and communal cleavages and disintegrations, underdevelopment and poverty and distributive Justice"[77.] The dynamics of these conflicts gravitate around what Edward Azar calls the "Core Identity" in African plural social systems dominated by primordial cleavages and sustained by prebendal and clientelistic competition for control of state instrumentalists for material patronage.[78] The consequent breakdown of civil order in extreme circumstances (Chad, Nigeria, Liberia, Togo, and Sierra Leone, etc.), derive from the over-politicization of the state as an organ to be monopolized for "absolute power and accelerated economic advancement"[79].

The structural roots of these malignant social conditions (to use Morton Deutsch category) reside invariably in three major contradictions in the social systems of African societies. One such contradiction relates to the history and nature of state formation in Africa as compared, for instance, to its counterpart in the West. Another contradiction derives from the 'pattern of elite recruitment and regime establishment and maintenance'. The implication of this factor for security is presently seen in the crisis of regime - legitimacy in a number of West African countries: Doe's Liberia, Cote d'Ivoire, Guinea Bissau, and Sierra Leone. The dynamics of this crisis are primarily anchored to exploitative relations at home and extreme dependence on external powers for political and economic sustenance by African countries.

Regarding the first issue-area (contraction arising from the history and nature of state formation in West Africa) it is often asserted that the low level of structural and value integration is positively associated with civil disorder in African states. Low-levels of structural and value integration productive of civil disorder in the West African region are often seen as concomitants of communication gaps, mass-elite dichotomy, limited degree of centralization and value congruence (pluralism) in these social formations. In other words, the greater the integration between structural elements in the system, the less likely is it that civil disorder would ensue.

Based on this conclusion, several theorists of "political violence and revolution" in Africa have sought to develop a general model of the "determinants of state violence that takes into account not only the character of challenges but a number of other historical, structural, and situational factors". Gurr has argued, for instance, that:

> Structural and cultural factors both shape general disposition to action, which in turn lead to strategic decisions about campaigns of political action. The actions and responses of regimes and challenges are both influenced by the same general structural and cultural constraints. The character of their actions and responses determines the nature of the conflict episode as well as its outcomes - reform, repression, revolution, or nothing.[80]

The structural and historical roots of these situational factors reside in the formative process of the African milieu compared with the European experience.

Thus, in the context of these overbearing realities in the region, analytical perspectives and prognosis (such as modernization and Marxism) which viewed ethnicity as "an evanescent, retrograde phenomenon" that would either give way under the "imperatives of development" or "ultimately be transcended by class solidarity", have proven largely predictively irrelevant. One general problem with this genre of conflict theory is its invariant focus on the internal dynamics of the social order to the exclusion of the "international linkages and constraints that shape internal conflict - an omission that is especially important in the African setting"[81] In other words, the paradigm of discourse in this mode of analysis is state-centric, historical and mechanistic in orientation.

A composite understanding of the generative structure of domestic disorder in the West African sub-region must necessarily take into cognizance, the important roles played by external factors in promoting or mediating those conflicts. According to Theda Skocpol[82], these include:

i) External capitalist penetration into rural economies and the consequent effects of agricultural commercialization on class conflict in pre-revolutionary states;

ii) Dependency on foreign trade, capital, and technology, which tends to "restrict the state's policy options, stimulate the growth of a dependent bourgeoisie aligned with international rather than national interests, and require authoritarian pattern of rule and reliance on coercion to protect the interests of international capital and its local clients" (petrobusiness in Nigeria and the Diamond Industry in Sierra Leone); and

iii) International political pressure, including foreign military threats, intervention, and alliance involvements, "all of which tend to increase the state's allocation of resources to military purposes, increase hostile external support for opposition movements, and reduce the state's freedom of political manoeuvre with respect to opposition".

Thus, an adequate explanatory model of the problematique of civil war in West Africa must broaden its factorial system (system of variables) beyond the nation - state as a unit of analysis and seek to integrate exogenous variables which condition internal processes of social change in the polity.

From the standpoint of conflict interaction in the region, one cannot fully comprehend the domestic sources of regional insecurity if different societies are treated as isolated artifacts from the prevailing structures of regional and global systems. In this regard, conflict spiral in the region could

64

be treated as an antagonistic situation in which influences from all levels interact over time. By identifying linkages among individual, societal and systemic variables, the dimensions and complexities of conflict situations can be highlighted. Within such analytical framework, the immediate task becomes to isolate: i) the environmental variables (long-term contextual and convergent; medium-term and precipitating factors) that contribute to conflict development in African social systems, and ii) the systemic factors that sustain them.

As manifested over the past four decades, the former (environmental variables include volitional factors such as "discontents, cultural and ideological dispositions, and rational choices in the making of political violence and revolutions", structural factors such as "tensions created by patterns of social relations") and political process variables such as the characteristics of political institutions and those who challenge them". In general terms, as they structure the genesis and trajectory of domestic conflict, these variables range from societal fragmentation (ethnic pluralism), fissiparous pressures towards secession to colonial legacies of arbitrary borders and configuration of elite power groups. The dynamics of such elite economic, political and ideological configuration (as will be seen below) provide the context for escalation of domestic disputes into civil wars.

Nevertheless, in generative terms, as the post-Cold War tendencies in the sub-region suggest (Liberia, Togo, Sierra Leone, Nigeria) the form, intensity, and potential effects of conflict episodes have their genesis in group mobilization involving "several overlapping identities: ethnicity and class, class and political association, ethnicity and political association - sometimes all three."[83] Causes and processes of conflict in West Africa are also often seen to vary as the bases of group mobilization and are sensitive to the specificities of African societies and regimes: the extent of intergroup inequalities, patterns of ethnic dominance, and the kinds of conflict - minimizing policies followed by states". These precipitants combine with

65

communal, political, and emerging class bases of identification interact to shape and reshape patterns of conflict in the sub-region.

The preceding discourse on the history and nature of state formation in West Africa saddled the second contradiction: the "pattern of elite recruitment and regime establishment and maintenance" in post-colonial Africa is in itself a result ("reproduction") of the "articulation" process in the "making of the "Third World" societies[84]. The crucial characteristics of this relationship have been "lopsided interdependencies". This essentially exploitative relationship is in turn anchored primarily to class structures and prostrate external dependence sustained by obtuse security system relations, which during the French presence in West Central Africa provide a graphic example. Thus, as Robert Fatton incisively argues:

> The frailty of the ruling classes is directly related to the peripheral nature of African societies. The dependent and backward character of African capitalism has contributed to the material and hegemonic frailty of most African bourgeoisies and thus to authoritarian political forms of governance. Such authoritarian forms, however, mask the Ruling classes 'relative incapacity to transform their power into effective political, economic, and cultural policies[85]

In these circumstances, the state in West Africa "embodies the contradictions of ruling": 'the African ruling classes' incapacity to transform effectively their state power into class power has created the "terrain for violent and often mutually destructive confrontations between contending fractions vying for domination". In this instance, the "state may move toward autonomization to prevent the catastrophic explosion of internecine class struggles resulting from the absence of a hegemonic class power".[86.] Thus, the African state does not have organic linkages between the political society, on the one hand, and civil society on the other. An 'integral state' in Gramscian discourse is basically a hegemonic state to the extent that hegemony implies "consent rather than domination, integration rather than exclusion, and co-optation rather than suppression":

A ruling class is hegemonic when it has established both its material dominance and its intellectual and moral leadership over society and when it succeeds in persuading subaltern classes that position of subordination and super-ordination are just, proper, and legitimate. This requires that the ruling class be prepared to make certain concessions, which, while not fundamental, contribute to the political co-optation of popular sectors and the progressive expansion of the productive process. This is the moment of "historic unity" when the ruling class has established its material, ethical, and political leadership over society and where the relationships of super-ordination and subordination are accepted by all as organic and not contradictory and as legitimate and not exploitative. When such a situation crystallizes, the ruling class has achieved what might be called paradigmatic hegemony.[87]

Generally, in the African condition, the absence of interest and value congruence between the "ruler and the ruled" has turned governance into a struggle for control of the state which in "conditions of monolithic political structures" (Niger, Togo, Cote d'Ivoire, Liberia) and generalized material scarcity, becomes "Hobbessian, violent, and deadly". In this enervating condition, social policies and the social order are "imposed by direct domination on those who do not consent either actively or passively to the rule of the governing classes"[88]. The inevitable consequence of such value dissensus and legitimacy crisis is the current and unprecedented turbulence in the structure of domestic power relations-from "consent under intimidation" to quest for popular sovereignty. The non-hegemonic status of African elites has engendered an existential condition in which the "rule of most African ruling classes is authoritarian, brutal and violent." In Nigeria, under the military Junta and in Liberia under Doe, compliance was the result of coercion and not consensus", and popular resistance gathered momentum in the past decade. The dynamics of governance, therefore, gravitate around the primitive accumulation of capital. Irving Markovitz explains why:

Class power in Africa is fundamentally dependent on state power. Capturing the state is the best and perhaps exclusive means for acquiring and generating the material wealth necessary for becoming a ruling class. The absence of a hegemonic African bourgeoisie, grounded in a solid and independent economic base successfully engaged in the private accumulation of capital, has transformed politics into material struggle. State Power provides the fundamental opportunity to build class power in a context of great and increasing scarcity. Not surprisingly, once an incipient ruling class takes over the state, it monopolizes it for its exclusive material and political gain and uses it for the violent exclusion of potential rival groups[106].

The extreme manifestations of this travail of political power and its attendant excesses have been the violent collapse of civil order in Liberia, Sierra Leone, Guinea Bissau and Chad, and the emergence of a malignant social condition of insecurity breeding disorder, and repression as the leaders were bent on staying power to the exclusion of others by all means. The irrepressible challenge to monopoly of the state by the dominant fraction of African elite is now the leitmotif of the democratic revolt and movements seeking to end decades of degenerate despotic rule.

Although these agitations have taken various forms and also registered divergent degrees of success depending on the specificity of local conditions, their root causes and express goal have been observably the same:

Spawned by shifting political authoritarianism and economic decay, and triggered by the spectacle of the fall of titans in Bucharest and elsewhere, in 1990 a powerful backwash of popular demonstrations for 'redemocratization' flooded all tidal wave, methodically transforming the political map of the continent.... The call for democracy was not just for a charter of the state, underpinned by political liberalism and accountability.[89]

68

By fundamentally disrupting the structures of domination-gerontocracy, patriarchy, clientelism, patrimonialism and corporatism which exist in a "variety of forms of articulation with each other" - the democratization process has engendered favourable conditions for the reverse of the suffocation of civil society "which has characterized political competition and political relations in Africa" for the past three decades.[90] It is in this domain that the current debate about civil society and democratization in Africa finds its provenance. Thus, in the emerging conditions of the 1990s and 21st Century, any conception of security that ignores the multiform structure of the state and society is necessarily emasculated.

2.6 Conclusion

In the increasingly variegated and complex African arena conditioned by the double antimony of systemic pressures (adjustment and transformation) and massive internal opposition from popular forces, the structural and distributive direction of state policies in the region have grave potentials for the security of the core and context - specific values of the society. The consequences of internal convulsion, as seen in Sierra Leone, Liberia and Chad, have been a further process of fragmentation of state and security relations as the emerging social forces challenge the state to the monopoly of the instruments of coercion or force. This changing social context in the continent has generated animated debates concerning issues of democracy and security has argued for instance, that in the light of the current development in the continent, "democratization and nation-building" have proven "antithetical in circumstances of ethnic diversity". Thus nation-building projects initiated by African states in the post-1945 period have recorded very little success mainly because the democracy in most cases simply facilitated the creation of ethnically centred political parties and associations. Given the intractability of domestic factors, which generate and fuel conflict and confrontation, the prevailing condition of insecurity in the West African sub-region will likely continue in the foreseeable future.

Against such a background of "internal legitimacy voids, and changed societal forces", the multiplicity of communal and mass violence in an essentially praetorian condition will continue to structure social relations and conflict conditions as the prebendal actors pursue their interests through the means of the state. The state is thus instrumental and also expresses the terrain of social conflict, domination and control. In terms of its "materialization" and "condensation", prevailing conflict over state power in the sub-region gravitates around ethnic, class, regional and religious identities as could be seen in the politics of exclusion in Cote d'Ivoire. As Otwin Marenin explains:

> These general conditions provide the environment for three trends in changing patterns of power and conflict, that is, in the nature of conflict coalitions and the forms of the state: the consolidation of a political class, a conflict coalition which, though the specific coalition partners change, has successfully neutralized competing class forces and ideological rivals, the centralization of state power, and the persistence and even resurgence of ethnic sentiments[91].

Thus, as Young has incisively argued, the "definition of groups is in constant flux; any theory of ethnic conflict must incorporate change as a central element" [92]. This is so because "political events are an important independent variable in determining the salience of cultural conflicts at any moment in time. At one moment, ethnic conflicts may appear to eclipse all other factors in the political equation; a few years later, the same cleavage may appear entirely muted," and quite irrelevant to "explication of the political process." Hence, the terrain of conflict can vary, as in Nigeria, from the extreme ethnic animosity of the 1960s and 1970s to the ideological contestation against military tyranny epitomized by National Democratic Coalition, NADECO, and in the current context, the resurgence of religious fundamentalism as an organizing principle (in terms of behavioural code) for political power symbolized in the epiphany of Sharia. However, in terms of future prospects for conflict management and resolution in the

West African sub-region, politicized ethnic sentiment (in Liberia, Nigeria, Cote d'Ivoire, Sierra Leone and Chad) remain the most deadly force in "Africa's syncretic, marginal, non-nation states with all its deleterious and negative effects."[93]

This imminent disposition in the African region finds its ideological reinforcement in the global-ethno political conflict given incisive articulation in Samuel Huntington's the **Clash of Civilization**. According to him,

The fundamental source of conflict in this new world will not be primarily ideological or primarily economic. The great divisions among human kind and the dominating source of conflict will be cultural. Nation states will remain the most powerful actors in world affairs, but the principal conflicts of global politics will occur between nations and groups of different civilizations. The fault lines between civilizations will be the battle lines of the future. In this emerging global trend, Huntington concludes, the "most pervasive, important, and dangerous conflicts will not be between social classes, rich and poor, or other economically defined groups, but between peoples belonging to different cultural entities". [94.]

Although Huntington's thesis has been the subject of extensive debate and criticism, the terrain of social conflict and group mobilization (social forces) is increasingly defined by cultural boundaries. In this regard, the politics of confrontation and accommodation in Nigeria, for instance, is structured less by the formal institutions of political parties than by dominant social forces, representing the tripolar character of its social formation: the Arewa Consultative Forum (predominantly, Hausa/Fulani), the Ohaneze (Igbo) and the Afenifere (Yoruba). Whether the multi-nation state of Nigeria remains or breaks in future, will depend on the reciprocal perceptions and actions of these social forces and the extent to which the State (the Federal Government) can contain the recurring riots and communal violence unleashed by their respective ethnic militias: the Oodua People's Congress,

OPC, the Arewa People's Congress, APC and the Bakassi Boys and Movement for the Actualization of the Sovereign State of Biafra, MASSOB.

This ethnic centrifugence underscores the generative source of the fundamental variation of civil war in West Africa before 1990 and after. While the dominant trend in the decades before the end of the Cold-War assumed the form of armed challenges by ethnic militants against a *de facto* entity (the state) in the form of war of secession (Nigeria), irredentism (Ghana-Togo), and the general onslaught on the authoritarian, decrepit and moribund state (Chad), the post-1990 period has seen protracted social conflicts arising from the collapse of neopatrimonial regimes (Liberia, and Sierra Leone), the retreat of extra-continental interests and forces (interventionism), and the employment of "what some perceive as novel warfare strategies", child combatants, mercenaries, ethnic cleansing and atrocities against defenseless civilians, such as the brutal amputations perpetrated by the RUF lumpen militias. As argued above, this phenomenon is not only limited to Africa, but expresses an emerging trend in the context of global ethnopolitical conflicts from Columbia and Mexico to the killing fields of the Middle East and Afghanistan, to the mayhem of Indonesia and the Philippines archipelago. As Foulie Psalidas-Perlmutter puts it:

> The quest for ethnic identity and the ensuing internal, personal, and intragroup turbulence may be as ancient as human history. However, it seems that…Such conflicts have become the basis of human and "political fault lines in the modern World". Following certain ideas of Herbert Kelman one can underline the internal contradictions of what he calls "ethno-national identity groups". They may serve certain basic psycho-sociological human needs for the sense of "being" for belonging, for generational, traditional, cultural and historical continuity. However, identity-driven political struggles can also provoke a destructive sense of "otherness" and hostility towards other groups

that have similar needs, but which originated and developed in a different context[95].

This factor has arguably become the bane of West African countries as politically driven ethnic turbulence threatens the stability of the nascent democratic experiments in the sub-region. With the erosion of ideologies (Socialism, Nationalism, Populism) as the source of political legitimacy, primordial identities such as ethnicity and religion, is becoming the dominant force in the "action-set" (political arena) of these countries. By creating "vertical links across class strata (e.g. through patron-client networks, political graft, and resource allocation)", the politics of prebendalism help to "maintain a level of integration quite out of proportion to objective class differences, which in weak states are often severe". This pattern, as noted above, is reinforced in conditions in which "ethnic consciousness is already well developed, and ethnic mobilization is always likely to be successful and there is only a rudimentary development of secondary associations"[96]

Thus, in terms of future prospects for conflict management and resolution in the sub-region, politicized ethnic sentiment remains the most deadly force. As Stephen Stedman observes, "the wars of the 1990s confirm a basic finding from the study of civil war termination: "peacemaking is a risky business".[97] The greatest source of risk comes from spoiler-leaders and parties who believe that "peace emerging from negotiations threatens their power, worldview, and interests, and use violence to undermine attempts to achieve it". As a number of episodes from the African tragedy (Angola in 1992, Rwanda in 1994 and Burundi in 2001) suggest that, when "spoilers succeed, the results are catastrophic". If, in the immediate future, however, contestants in the power game in the exploding "African flashpoints" dread the "implications of a showdown more than they value the possibilities of winning engagements", then the basis of accommodation or conflict settlement might be a distinct possibility as in Liberia or Sierra Leone. The tragedy, however is that the zero-sum nature of the power contest combined with "persevering economic decay" against backgrounds of psychologically heightened expectations may continue to produce explosive results. As Chase-Dunn reminds us, "the key truth about politics-morally, practically, theoretically-is always that matters could have been different." [98]

Notes and References

1. Shaw, T. (1994) "The South in the New World (Dis) Order: Towards a Political Economy of Third World Foreign Policy in the 990s", *Third World Quarterly Vol.* 15, No. 1 (1994): 17-30
2. Rondos, A. (1996) "The Collapsing State and International Security" in E. Kolodziej and K. Roger, **Coping with Conflict After the Cold War,** Baltimore: John Hopkins University Press, 489.
3. Jackson, R. (2001) "The State and Internal Conflict", Australian Journal of *International Affairs,* vol. 55, No. 1, 2001: 67.
4. Kolodziej and Zartman, W. (1996) "Coping with Conflict: A Global Approach" in E. Kolodziej and R.Kanet, **Coping with Conflict After the Cold War,** Baltimore: John Hopkins University Press, 13.
5. Gantzel, K. (1997) "War in the Post-World War II World: Some Empirical Trends and Theoretical Approach" in D. Turton (ed.), **War and Ethnicity: Global Connections and Local Violence,** Rochester, N.Y: University of Rochester Press, 139
6. Conteh-Morgan, E. (1993), "Conflict and Militarialization in Africa: Past trends and New Scenarios", *Conflict Quarterly.* Winter, 1993: 28
7. Kolodziej and Zartman, W. (1996) "Coping with Conflict: A Global Approach" in E. Kolodziej and R.Kanet, **Coping with Conflict After the Cold War,** Baltimore: John Hopkins University Press, 14
8. Sandole, D. and Sandole, S. (1986) **Conflict Management and Problem Solving: Interpersonal to International Approach,** London: Frances Pinter, 35
9. Ross, (1993) **The Culture of Conflict,** New Haven: Yale University Press, 18

10. Ayoob, M. (1996) **Regional Security and the Third World,** London: Croom Helm, 7

11. George, J. (1986) "Mechanisms for Moderating Superpowers Competition", AEI *Foreign Policy and Defence Review* 1986: 7

12. Ake, C., (1985); "The Future of the State in Africa", *International Political Science Review Vol. 6,* No. 1: 105

13. ____(2001) **Democracy and Development in Africa,** Ibadan, Spectrum Books, 33

14. Conteh-Morgan, E. (1993), "Conflict and Militarization in Africa: Past Trends and New Scenarios", *Conflict Quarterly,* Winter, 1993: 28

15. Kaldor, M (1999) **New and Old Wars: Organized Violence in a Global Era,** Cambridge: Polity Press, 1-3

16. Kaplan, D. (1994) "The Coming Anarchy: How Scarcity, Crime, Overpopulation and Diseases are Rapidly Destroying the Social Fabric of our Planet", *Atlantic Monthly,* February; 47

17. Kaldor, M (1999) **New and Old Wars: Organized Violence in a Global Era,** Cambridge: Polity Press, 1-3

18. Snyder, L "Political Disintegration in Developing Countries: Theoretical Orientation and Empirical Evidence", *International Interactions* vol. 11, No. 2: 137-166.

19 Kaufman, S. (1996) "Spiraling to Ethnic War", *International Security 21*: 108-138.

20. Ayoob, M. (1996) **Regional Security and the Third World,** London: Croom Helm, 7

21. Jackson, Robert (1990) **Quasi-States: Sovereignty, International Relations, and the Third World,** New York: Cambridge University Press, 69

22. Ibid, 69

23. Ibid; 70.

24. Abdullah, I.,(1997); "Bush Path to Destruction: The Origin and Character of the Revolutionary United Front, RUF", 17

25. Bangura et al.. (1977); "Lumpen Youth Culture and Political Violence: Sierra Leoneans Debate on the RUF and the Civil War", *Africa Development* Vol. XXII, Nos. ¼ 171.

26. Honwana, A. (1999) "Negotiating Post-War Identities: Child Soldiers in Mozambique and Angola", *CODESRIA Bulletin 1* and 2, 1999: 6

27. Ibid; 6

28. Vine, A. (1991) **Renamo: Terrorism in Mozambique**, London: Centre for Southern African Studies, University Press, 95-96

29. Bangura et al., (1977); "Lumpen Youth Culture and Political Violence: Sierra Leoneans Debate on the RUF and the Civil War", *Africa Development* Vol. XXII, Nos. 3&4, 173.

30. Ibid; 203

31. Rummel, R. (1966) "Dimensions of Conflict Behaviour Within Nations", *Journal of Conflict Resolution* 10 (March, 1966): 65

32. Gurr, T. (1970) **Why Men Rebel**, Princeton: Princeton University Press.

33. Rosenau, J. (1996) **Turbulence in World Politics**, Princeton: Princeton University Press, 268

34. Elbadawi, I. and Sambanis, N. (2000), "Why are there so many Civil Wars in Africa? Understanding and Preventing Violent Conflict", *Journal of African Economics,* 9,3, October 2000: 244-.

35. Snyder, L "Political Disintegration in Developing Countries: Theoretical Orientation and Empirical Evidence", *International Interactions* Vol. 11, No. 2: 154

36. Azar, E., (1990); **The Management of Protracted Social Conflict: Theory and Cases,** Aldershot: Darmouth Publishing Company, 25.

37. Scaritt, J. (1993) "Communal Conflict and Contention for Power in Africa South of the Sahara" in T. Gurr (ed.), Minorities at Risk, Washington, DC: United States Peace Institute Press, 253

38. I bid; 252

39. For more on this, see Young, C. (1982) "Patterns of Social Conflict: State, Class, and Ethnicity", *Daedalus* 3 (1982), and Rothchild, D (1997) **Managing Ethnic Conflict in Africa**, Washington, D.C. Brookings Institution, 13

40. Scaritt, J. op. cit; 253

41. Gurr, T. (1991) "Theories of Political Violence and Revolution in the Third World", in F. Deng and W. Zartman, (1991)(eds.) **Conflict Resolution in Africa**, Washington, D.C The Brookings Institution, 168.

42. Barraclough, G., (1977); **Introduction to Contemporary History**, Hammondsworth: Penguin, 191

43. Gurr, T. (1991), op. cit, 168.

44. For more on this, see Rothchild, D. (1991) "An Interactive Model for State-Ethnic Relations" in Deng F. and Zartman (1991)(eds.) **Managing Ethnic Conflict in Africa**, Washington DC. Brookings Institution, And Young, C. (1982) "Patterns of Social Conflict: State, Class, and Ethnicity", Daedalus 3 (1982).

45. For details, see Amadu Sesay, "The Limits of Peace-keeping by Regional Organization: The OAU Peacekeeping Force in Chad", in *Conflict Quarterly,* Fredericton, Vol. X1, Vol.1, winter 1991, 7-26 and Amadu Sesay, "The OAU Peacekeeping Force in Chad: Some Lessons for the Future", in *Current Research on Peace and Violence*, Tampere, Finland, Vol.X11, No. 4, 1989, 191-200

46. Mukonoweshuro, E. (1993) Colonialism, **Class Formation and Underdevelopment in Sierra Leone**, Lanham: Falmer, and Richards, P. Richard, P. (1995) " The War in Liberia and Sierra Leone", in Oliver Furley (ed,) **Conflcit in Africa**, London: Heinemann.

47. Rummel, R. (1966) "Dimensions of Conflict Behaviour Within Nations", *Journal of Conflict Resolution* 10 (March, 1966): **65-73**

48. Huntington, S. (1972) **Political Order in Changing Societies**, N.Y: Yale University Press, 194

49. Rule, J. (1988) **Theories of Civil Violence**, Berkeley: University of California.

50. See Zartman, I. W. (ed.) (1993), **Negotiating Internal Conflicts,** Columbia: University of South Carolina Press, and Zartman, I.W. (1995)(ed.), **Negotiating an End to Civil Wars,** Washington, D.C. The Brookings Institution

51. Chilcote, R., (1981), **Theories of Comparative Politics,** Boulder: Westview, 74.

52. Huntington, S. (1972) **Political Order in Changing Societies,** N.Y: Yale University Press, 29.

53. Reno, W. (1995) **Warlord Politics and African States,** Boulder Lynne Rienner, 75.

54. For details, see, Young, C. (1993) **The Politics of Cultural Pluralism,** Wisconsin: The University of Wisconsin Press.

55. Jackson, R. and Rosberg, C. (1982) "Why Africa's Weak States Persist: The Empirical and the Juridical Statehood", *World Politics* 35:1-24, and   Brown, M. (ed.) (1996); **The International Dimensions of Internal Conflict,** Cambridge, Mass: Center for Science and International Affairs.

56. Mueller, J. (2000) "The Banality of Ethnic War", *International Security* vol. 25, No.1. (Summer 2000): 42-70, and Herbst, J. (1996/7) " Responding to State Failure in Africa", *International Security,* 21:120-144.

57. Elbadawi, I. and Sambanis, N. (2000), "Why are there so many Civil Wars in Africa? Understanding and Preventing Violent Conflict", *Journal of African Economics,* 9,3, October 2000: 225.

58. Ibid; 259.

59. Ibid; 225.

60. Rothchild, D. (1997), **Managing Ethnic Conflict in Africa,** Washington, D.C.; The Brooking Institution, 198.

61. Ibid; 198

62. Ibid; 199.

63. Marenin, O. (1987) "The Managerial State in Africa: A Conflict Coalition Perspective" in Z. Ergas (ed.), **The African State in Transition,** N.Y: St. Martin, 216.

64. Markowitz, I. (1987) **Studies in Power and Class in Africa**, N.Y.: Oxford University Press, 62.
65. Rothchild, D. and Growth A. (1995), "Pathological Dimensions of Domestic and International Ethnicity" *Political Science Quarterly* 110, 1 (Spring, 1995)
66. Duffield, M. (1998), "Post-Modern Conflict: Warlords, Post-Adjustment States and Private Protection", *Civil War* 1:67
67. Ibid; 67
68. Roxborough, I. (1979) **Theories of Underdevelopment**, London: Macmillan, 25, and Chase-Dunn, D (1992), **Global Formation**, Cambridge Mass: Westview, for more details on this subject, 25.
69. Ibid; 49.
70. Gantzel. K (1997), " War in the Post-World War II World; Some Empirical Trends and Theoretical Approaches", op. cit. 139
71. Mujaju, A., (1989) "International Conflict and Its International Context" in K. Rupesinghe (ed.), **Conflict Resolution in Uganda,** London: James Currey, 260.
72. For more on this, see Diamond, L. (1989) "Beyond Autocracy: Prospects for Democracy in Africa" in **Beyond Autocracy in Africa,** Atlanta: The Carter Center of Emory University, and Migdal, J. (1988) **Strong Societies and Weak States: State-Society Relations and State Capabilities in the Third World,** Princeton: Princeton University Press, 21
73. Onimode, B. (1988) **The Political Economy of the African Crises,** London: Zed, 2, and Fatton, R. (1988) "Bringing the Ruling Class Back in: Class, State and Hegemony in Africa", *Comparative Politics*, April 1988:253-264
74. Sangmpam, S.N. (1993) "Neither Soft Nor Dead: The African State is Alive and Well", *African Studies Review,* vol. 36, No.2, September, 1993: 35.
75. Diamond, L. (1989) "Beyond Autocracy: Prospects for Democracy in Africa" in **Beyond Autocracy in Africa,** Atlanta: The Carter Center of Emory University, 21.

76. Zartman, I.W. (ed.) (1995) **Negotiating an End to Civil Wars,** Washington, D.C. The Brookings Institution.

77. Ayoob, M. (1996) **Regional Security and the Third World,** London: Croom Helm

78. Azar, E., (1990); **The Management of Protracted Social Conflict: Theory and Cases,** Aldershot: Darmouth Publishing Company, 25.

79. Fatton, R. (1988) "Bringing the Ruling Class Back in: Class, State and Hegemony in Africa", *Comparative Politics*, April 1988:255.

80. Gurr. T. (1991) "Theories of Political Violence in the Third World", Op. cit; 178

81. Snow, D. (1996) **Uncivil Wars: International Security and New International Conflicts,** Boulder: Lynne Rienner, 47.

82. See Skocpol, T (1979) **States and Revolution: A Comparative Analysis of France, Russia and China,** N.Y: Cambridge University Press.

83. Gurr, T. (1993) **Minorities at Risk: A Global View of Ethno-political Conflicts,** Washington, D.C: United States Institute of Peace Press.

84. Poulantzas, N. (1978) **Political Power and Social Classes,** London Verso Editions.

85. Fatton, R. (1988) "Bringing the Ruling Class Back in: Class, State and Hegemony in Africa", *Comparative Politics,* April 1988:225.

86. Marenin, O. (1987) "The Managerial State in Africa: A Conflict Coalition Perspective" in Z. Ergas (ed.), **The African State in Transition,** N.Y: St. Martin, 217

87. Miliband, R. (1983) **Class Power and State Power,** London: Verso Editions, 26.

88. Young,C. "Patterns of Social Conflict: State, Class and Ethnicity" *Daedalus* 3, 13

89. Markovitz, I, op. cit. 8.

90. Decalo, S. (1992), " The Process, Prospects and Constraints of Democratization in Africa", *African Affairs* 91 (1992): 7-8.
91. Marenin, op. cit; 111
92. Young, "Patterns of Social Conflict: State, Class and Ethnicity" *Daedalus* 3, 13
93. Diamond, L (1989) "Beyond Autocracy: Prospects for Democracy in Africa", in **Beyond Autocracy in Africa**, Atlanta: The Carter Centre of Emory University, 24.
94. Huntington, S. (1997) **The Clash of Civilizations and the Remaking of World Order,** NY: Simon and Schuster, 28.
95. Psalidas-Perlmutter, F. (2000) "The Interplay of Myths and Realities", *Orbis,* Spring 2000: 237.
96. Jackson, R (2001), "The State and Internal Conflict", *Australian Journal of International Affairs*, Vol. 55. No. 1, 2001, 72-73
97. Stedman, S.J. (1997) "Spoiler Problems in Peace Processes", *International Security* Vol. 22, No. 2, (1997): 5.
98. Chase-Dunn, (1992), **Global Formation,** Cambridge Mass: Blackwell. 214

Section Three: The Geopolitics of Civil Wars in the Mano River Union

Chapter Three: State Disintegration and Civil War in Liberia

Charles Ukeje

3.1 Introduction

Liberia, the first de facto independent state in the continent of Africa was embroiled in a catastrophic civil war that started on the eve of Christmas in 1989,when its north-eastern border region with Cote d'Ivoire, was attacked by a handful of dissident rebels under the National Patriotic Front of Liberia (NPFL). The incursion, initially claimed by the government of Samuel Kanyon Doe to be a minor border skirmish, gradually grew to become one of the most protracted domestic armed insurrections ever to break out in the sub-region of West Africa. The civil war 'ended' after seven years of frustrating intransigence on the part of the major actors eventually paved the way for a comprehensive ceasefire and general elections in July 1997 which were, as expected, won by the leader of the NPFL rebel group, Charles Taylor.

The new political dispensation after the first post-war elections and Taylor's inauguration was, of course, a welcome respite- first, for the citizens who survived the harrowing atrocities committed by the different warring factions, and second, for the ECOWAS Member States who invested heavily in diplomatic, financial, military and humanitarian resources to achieve peace and stability for that country against all odds. At the same time, however, the sad reality was never lost on stakeholders within and outside Liberia that the dividends of peace supposedly achieved might not stand the stringent test of time, especially going by the character of the successor regime and the style of governance of President Taylor. Predictably, those who expressed this cautious optimism won the day as Liberia relapsed again, into another vicious cycle of civil war instigated by a new group of dissidents under the banner of Liberians United for Reconstruction and Development (LURD), most of whom felt alienated from the wobbling post-war reconstruction, rehabilitation and reconciliation agenda of the Taylor regime. Undoubtedly, the resumption of armed hostilities in already war-ravaged Liberia since late 2000 is a direct carry-over from the ignored and/ or unfinished businesses of the earlier civil war.

The literature on the Liberian civil war is already a huge industry. Thus in this chapter, emphasis is placed on providing critical insights that illuminate the unique elements and dimensions of the civil war that threatened the stability and survival of the Liberian State on the one hand, and tasked the politico-diplomatic, military and economic capabilities of Member States of the ECOWAS on the other. The first section traces the prelude to the first civil war just before Liberia began a steady but inexorable socio-economic decline and political disintegration. That difficult period coincided with the groundswell of civil society-embedded opposition groups inside and outside the country that eventually provided the cesspool from which the rebel groups drew their loyalists and foot soldiers. The second section explores the novel dimensions and impacts of the Liberian civil war, while the third examines the long and seemingly intractable search for peace, especially but not exclusively under the framework of ECOWAS. The fourth section suggests that the character of the post-war regime of Charles Taylor, particularly his reluctance to make the much-expected transition from a warlord to a respectable statesman and president is the single most formidable stumbling block to reconstruction, rehabilitation and reconciliation in Liberia. Indeed, as this chapter argues, what Liberia has enjoyed since Taylor was declared president in 1997, has always been a peace of the graveyard. The final section examines the current political situation in Liberia against the background of the resumption of another round of civil war instigated by LURD.

3.2 Historical and Contemporary Seeds of Social Disintegration and State Collapse in Liberia

Modern day Liberia is a creation of the American Colonization Society- a movement dedicated to the repatriation and resettlement of freed slaves in

Africa. From 1821 onwards, many of the freed black slaves from the United States of America were resettled in present day Liberia, and by 1847 this haven of 'free people of colour', became the Republic of Liberia. Although initially limited to the coastal areas, control was soon extended into the hinterlands from the 1890s through a consummate project of '*pax-Liberiana*', involving the military and political subjugation of indigenous peoples lasting well into the 1920s. Expectedly, this historical origin left an indelible mark on the country as virtually every aspect of national life was under the firm grip of the descendants of the settlers called Americo-Liberians, who constituted a tiny 4% of the country's population. Until the coup d'etat of 1980 that brought Sergeant Samuel Doe to power, there-fore, the political sphere was the exclusive preserve of the minority Americo-Liberians who enjoyed an uninterrupted rule spanning over 100 years under the tutelage of the True Whig Party (TWP). Predictably, unchal-lenged political dominance attracted and secured economic prosperity for the ruling class, just as it spawned an elaborate system of social and reli-gious patronage and clientelism beneficial almost exclusively to the Americo-Liberians. This infrastructure of power, control and domination ran side-by-side with that which was characterized by the subservience, marginalization and exclusion of the vast majority of the indigenous popu-lation[1]. The stability enforced by the minority Americo-Liberian ruling class in public and private spheres only suppressed but never completely wiped out counter-political discourse amongst indigenous elites. Indeed, there was a vibrant undercurrent of pent-up anger and frustration within the ranks of indigenous elite and peoples against this *black-on-black* colo-nialism[2]. Increasingly, this groundswell of frustration became more pro-nounced during the late 1970s with the economic downturn when the adverse effects of declining world demand for iron ore and rubber, two principal foreign exchange earners, resulted in a steep decline in the living standards and conditions of the vast majority of Liberians.

By 1979, there was a groundswell of radical opposition to the political orthodoxy as reflected, first, in the formation of the Progressive Alliance of Liberia (PAL) and later, the Progressive People's Party (PPP) both under the leadership of Baccus Matthews. The clock of militant opposition to Americo-Liberian rule began to tick louder until its ignoble termination in April 1980 during a coup by non-commissioned rank-and-files of the Armed Forces of Liberia (AFL) led by Master Sergeant Samuel Doe. Coming from a background of political misrule, economic disempowerment and long suffering, the popular expectation at the time of Doe's coup was that the termination of the Century-long Americo-Liberian rule would reverse, in the short run, the socio-economic and political misfortunes of Liberians and place the country on a sound footing. In less than one year, however, this excitement fizzled as Doe embarked on strikingly similar- if not worse- kinds of high-handed misrule that earned his predecessors' public wrath and opprobrium. For instance, he cleverly manipulated the main ruling organ of his regime, the People's Redemption Council (PRC) in order to ensure absolute power and authority for himself, suspended the constitution, proscribed multiparty politics, hounded opposition elements into forced exile, and publicly executed top officials of the previous administration. From 1981 onwards, he began to victimize members of the PRC with dissenting ideological views, and by August of the same year, executed five of the founding members on trumped-up charges of conspiracy and sedition.

It is instructive to recall that throughout the long years of Americo-Liberian misrule, and to some extent the plunder of the country, ethnicity was also a major factor that determined the allocation of social value, privilege, authority and resources. As noted earlier, this social cancer afflicted virtually every facet of the Liberian society. Under Doe, ethnicity even intensified, as the most significant determinant of access to and/or exclusion from political, social and economic opportunities. Ethnic fault-lines eventually fed into the animosity that accelerated social collapse and eventually plunged Liberia into a seven-year bloody civil war. For much of the lifespan of the Doe regime, a clear battle line was drawn between the Krahn ethnic group where Samuel Doe came from, and the alliance of Gio-Mano ethnic groups believed to be plotting his regime's violent overthrow. The latter ethnic groups were systematically targeted for marginalization, ethnic cleansing, and state-sponsored repression. In October of 1983, for instance, Doe accused the last of his colleagues that masterminded the 1980 coup, Brigadier General Thomas Quiwonkpa, of plotting against his government. He was dismissed from the PRC, harassed out of the country, and was to lead an abortive coup later in November 1985, during which he was captured, tortured and killed by Doe (His corpse was displayed in the main streets of Monrovia for 'doubting Thomases' to see). By January 1986, the political scheming of Doe reached full maturity culminating in his transformation from a military head of state to a civilian president. His suspicious 'victory' during the October 1985 presidential elections complicated the ethnic equation as it forced opposition elements to close ranks[3]. Expectedly, this 'change of wardrobe' did not only erode public trust but also confirmed Doe's insatiable appetite and lust for power. His divide-and-rule style of governance on the one hand benefited and endeared him to his ethnic kinsmen, the Krahn, while alienating those from other ethnic groups, especially the Gio and Mano tribes on the other. These festering political and ethnic fault-lines, coupled with crises associated with regime profligacy and poor management of the economy eventually provided the template on which the civil war was ignited.

3.3 Liberia: The Pains of an Uncivil War

Although the sub-region of West Africa has experienced pockets of civil protests and insurrections, large-scale civil wars are a rarity. Indeed, for all the three decades after many countries in the sub-region attained independence, the only major civil war followed the failed attempt by secessionist Biafra to excise itself from Nigeria in a bitter civil war between 1967 and 1970. Even then, the latter occurred at the height of the Cold

War rivalry between the two major superpowers, the USA and USSR. The widespread notion that the termination of the Cold War would considerably elongate the corridors of peace and security in Africa in particular, and in many developing countries in general, have been realized only in the breach. The unpleasant trajectories of the civil war in Liberia, and the enormity of humanitarian and collective security burdens it imposed on Member States of ECOWAS, are poignant indicators of this failed expectation. Earlier, the chapter alluded to the seething ethnic mistrust and animosity that characterized the Doe era. What should be added here, then, is the fact that the leader of the NPFL rebel group, Charles Taylor, also manipulated and exploited this volatile ethnic equation in order to strengthen his fighting corporation as witnessed by the large number of people who enrolled into his hitherto small band of rebels. It was reported that in less than six months after the NPFL began its incursion, Taylor had taken effective control of an estimated 95% of Liberian territory, and was laying siege for the prized trophy, Monrovia.

It is unequivocal that successive stages of the Liberian civil war were punctuated by heinous human rights infringements as well as unprecedented subversion of international norms of civility during combat, culminating in what is called the "uncivil war"[4]. All the warring factions tried to outsmart the other in several respects, most importantly, in terms of gaining access to natural resources necessary for funding personal ambitions and the war efforts, committing atrocities against unarmed civilians, and the wanton destruction of social facilities and infrastructures.[5] Alao and Olonisakin have argued that even if the role of natural resources as a primary cause of the Liberian conflict is not immediately evident, the same cannot be said about the role resources played in the course of the Liberian civil war[6]. According to them, two distinct groups- the warring factions and the peacekeeping mission- took active part in the struggle to control and plunder natural resources in Liberia in order to fund their rebel projects and war efforts. They estimated that Charles Taylor alone must have earned over

400 million USD per year from trade in natural resources (timber, diamond and iron ore) during the war between 1992-1996[7].

The civil war accelerated the decline of socio-economic conditions in Liberia. The Liberian economy was predominantly dependent on agriculture and mining for about 70% of the country's workforce in the pre-war years. The collapse of the global markets for the products meant further rise in the cost of living coupled with a ridiculously high rate of inflation that eroded the parity once enjoyed by the Liberian Dollar vis-à-vis the U.S. Dollar. The average income of civil servants during the civil war reached an all-time low of about 5 USD per month against around 200 USD in the pre-war years. By 1990, the price of the main staple, rice, had skyrocketed between 25-30 USD for a 100 lbs bag.[8]. Expectedly, it was only a matter of time before the socio-economic decline triggered persistent and intense social and political upheavals.

A report commissioned by CODESRIA/OXFAM-UK on 'Household Economy in Liberia' highlighted vividly the depth of social and economic malaise facing the Liberian state. According to Wolokorie[9], traditional Liberian household structures both rural and urban were severely weakened, while the subsistence sector, which previously accounted for about 70% of total household income, also suffered at least 80% destruction of its productive capacity. The cumulative impact of these deteriorating trends, then, is at the root of the difficulties faced by low-income households from whom most of the combatants were recruited, to effectively absorb and re-integrate the former fighters. That the demobilization and rehabilitation phases of the post-war order were poorly executed are clear tributes to the nagging social problem affiliated with the weak capacity of families and communities to effectively re-integrate former soldiers. The rapid urbanization that took place within the capital city, Monrovia, as a consequence of the civil war also further complicated the plight of low-income earners and households. Almost half of the country's population now resides in Monrovia, having fled the unsafe countryside during the civil war years. The import of this demographic explosion is far-reaching in terms of the pressure that is brought to bear on existing fragile social infrastructure and municipal services in the capital, especially, housing, portable water, electricity, motorable roads, educational facilities and health care delivery networks. Many of the social infrastructures have collapsed outright, while those fortunate to be functioning provide at best epileptic service. In Monrovia, as in other parts of the country, only an estimated 35% of pre-war health care facilities have been restored. Many people still lack access to basic, talk-less of qualitative, health care facilities. The same trend is visible in virtually every social sector, including education as many children of primary or secondary school age have found it difficult to learn either because they lack the wherewithal to do so, or because the educational facilities are in ruins.[10]

It is important to recall, therefore, that the civil war triggered the massive mobilization of civilian population in support of the war efforts of the major protagonists. By April 1994, then, only 1,447 of the estimated 60, 000 troops in Liberia had disarmed at the 11 official demobilization points[11]. The other rebel factions were much more reluctant in encamping and handing over their weapons, talk less of beginning the process of demobilization and reintegration into civil life. Thus, as at 1995-1996, innocent civilians were still massacred by unidentified armed groups, while hostilities between and among the warring factions did not abate. In April 1998, an inter-factional conflict broke out between forces loyal to the newly elected government of Charles Taylor against Roosevelt Johnson's supporters. It later degenerated into open armed hostilities between LPC and the AFL on the one hand, and the NPFL and ULIMO-J, on the other. As the conflict spread, it reached Mamba Point- the exclusive government reserved area where most embassies and foreign delegations are situated. While Johnson was out of the country to attend an emergency summit meeting in May 1996, the NPFL again launched a preemptive attack against his main base at Barclays Training Centre. These separate incidents brought in their wake new rounds of displacements of civilians, majority of whom were headed towards the Monrovia Free Port in a desperate bid to flee the fighting and the country.

The major offensive by the NPFL against ECOMOG positions in the outskirts of Monrovia in October 1992 altered the operational mandate of the latter from that of traditional peacekeeping to that of peace enforcement. The offensive was part of a last minute desperate attempt by the NPFL to gain control of the last trophy, the capital, long protected by the residue of the AFL and ECOMOG. Although it did not succeed in capturing Monrovia at that time, the NPFL succeeded in taking every other part of the country, including Robertsville International Airport. By January 1993, however, ECOMOG dislodged the NPFL from the suburbs of Monrovia, recaptured the airport, the Firestone rubber plantation at Harbel and the port of Buchanan. As fighting intensified, both parties committed gross human rights abuses and violations against unarmed civilians. In June of that year, for example, AFL soldiers reportedly killed more than 600 people that sought refuge in the compounds of the Harbel rubber plantation. Three months later, a UN investigation indicted the detachment of troops that committed this grave atrocity. Without exception, however, all the factions in the Liberian civil war engaged in this orgy of violent assaults against innocent and harmless civilians, including children and women, and in places considered inviolable such as churches, mosques, hospitals, convents, and embassy grounds. By the time hostilities ceased, the 2.5 million pre-war population of Liberia had been decimated by about 200, 000, while several more suffer acute physical, medical and emotional conditions.

3.4 From Bamako to Abuja: The Tortuous Search for Peace
The Liberian civil war lasted almost seven years due mainly to the intransigence of the various rebel groups, as much as the apathy of the international community to intervene earlier and decisively to stem this abyss of anarchy[12]. In that regard, several agreements were reached during

meetings held in various countries within the West African sub-region—Banjul, Yamoussoukro, Lome, Cotonou, Accra and Abuja, and in far away Geneva[13.] This search for peace however suffered several setbacks. One of the earliest false starts occurred in August 1990 when ECOWAS released a blueprint for peace that also made provision for Interim Government of National Unity (IGNU), to prepare Liberia for democratic elections. Apart from the fact that it was rather too hasty at that time, the blueprint clearly excluded leaders of the rebel factions in the process- even though at that time, Charles Taylor's NPFL already exercised de facto control of a significant portion of the country. The earlier agreements, especially that emanating from Yamoussoukro faltered also by naively excluding Sierra Leone and Guinea; two neighboring countries that where directly involved in and affected by the civil war in Liberia. Expectedly, the governments in Freetown and Conakry repudiated its outcomes almost as soon as they were made public. Both capitals were also irritated that Yamoussoukro was rather 'clever by half' in trying to undermine the pivotal role played by Nigeria in the resolution of the civil war, in preference for that of Cote d'Ivoire[14].

Taylor's refusal to abide by the provisions of the Yamoussoukro IV Accord of October 1991 providing for a timetable for the disarmament and encampment of the warring factions within 60 days from November 15, created another stalemate that eventually led to the emergence of two de facto governments: one in Monrovia headed by Amos Sawyer, the other in Gbarnga- 90 miles north of the capital- under Taylor. Much of these complications were carried over to the Geneva II peace conference of June 1993 when the various warring factions refused to agree on an acceptable formula for sharing political offices in a proposed transitional government, and the most viable strategy for complete disarmament. One of the last peace initiatives aimed at resolving the Liberian civil war was held in Abuja, Nigeria's capital, in August 1995. The meeting provided, among others, for an interim government, disarmament, demobilization and the holding of free and fair elections. For the first time, all the warring factions were represented and they all endorsed the outcome of the meeting[15]. Like past initiatives, however, the Abuja meeting almost faltered because the faction leaders soon after began to pursue a two-track strategy: one for peace, another for war. By this, the factional leaders pursued political solutions within the framework of the Council of State provided for in the Abuja Accord, but also continued the war in the countryside.

The common strand that resonated throughout the peace meetings included the need for the various warring factions to implement agreed ceasefires, encampment, demobilization and disarmament of their combatants, and to commit themselves to free and fair elections and their outcome. Until the last meeting held in Abuja in June 1997, each of the peace agreements floundered as the warring factions observed them more in their breach. One reason for the recurrent bickering could be traced to the deep mistrust and ill feelings each of the major rebel groups harbored towards one another. At the same time, none of the rebel groups had much confidence in the impartiality of the Nigeria-dominated ECOMOG, believing that it had its own sinister agenda.[16] This was certainly the feeling within the Taylor camp, which believed that ECOMOG was the only stumbling block delaying what ordinarily would have been an unhindered occupation of the Executive Mansion in Monrovia. Not far from the truth, also, was the realization that peace was virtually impossible without Charles Taylor who exercised effective control over much of the country. Levitt[17] has explained the difficulty of reaching an acceptable post-war peace and order in the absence of a trust-building mechanism in the pre-intervention stage of most civil wars. By this, he suggested that the pre-intervention stage in the case of the Liberian civil war was fundamentally flawed because the external intervener, ECOMOG, did not enjoy the trust and confidence of the warring factions in battle[18].

But this thesis is not sufficient in explaining the difficulties encountered in reaching an agreeable formula for peace in Liberia. It is also important to look into the external complications that hampered this search, most especially the fact that the outbreak of the civil war coincided with a most inauspicious time for the major powers, particularly the United States of America and its Western European allies. On the part of Washington D.C., Liberia lost its pride of place and geo-strategic importance soon after the termination of the Cold War. It will be recalled that while the Cold War lasted, Liberia was one of the few favorites of Washington D.C. in Africa. The West African country provided important aircraft landing facilities as well as a listening post for U.S. intelligence gathering capabilities; while economically, it was one of the principal suppliers of rubber to the United States from the Firestone Plantation- at one time, the largest in the world. In return, Liberia attracted substantial financial concessions from the United States- much of which went towards shoring up the highly repressive and vindictive regime of Samuel Doe. All that effervesced after the Cold War as witnessed in the closing of the satellite tracking station and the change of ownership of the Firestone plantation.

By the time the Liberian civil war broke out, Washington was mainly preoccupied with the evacuation of its citizens and those of other European nations. Unlike the United States, Western European countries maintained a far limited presence in Liberia, much of which never surpassed symbolic diplomatic representation and minor commercial interests. More importantly, however, the outbreak of the Liberian civil war coincided with the upheavals in the former communist strongholds in Eastern Europe, particularly Yugoslavia. Most governments in Europe considered the civil wars in their backyards to be of higher priority than those in 'far away lands'. It did not come as a surprise, then, that it was only in late 1993, almost three years into the fiercest stage of the Liberian civil war, that some tokenish international effort, under the auspices of the United Nations, was put in place in Liberia.[19]

Virtually left in the lurch by the United States and major European countries; and for a long time by the United Nations, the burdensome responsibility of external intervention to manage attendant humanitarian emergencies fell on the weak shoulders of a few Member States of ECOWAS- notably Ghana, Guinea, Sierra Leone, the Gambia, and Nigeria- who pioneered what has become a unique and unparalleled sub-regional peacekeeping and peace-enforcement initiative under the aegis of ECOMOG, the ECOWAS Monitoring Group.[20] Although the initial phase of this sub-regional mediation and peacekeeping intervention was punctuated by rancorous disagreements, particularly by Cote d'Ivoire and Burkina Faso who were deeply suspicious of the Nigeria-led venture, the distrust never deterred the members of the ECOWAS Standing Mediation Committee (SMC), from intensifying the search for peace.[21] At the Summit of ECOWAS held in Banjul, the Gambia, in May 1990, the SMC proposed that ECOMOG[22] forces be dispatched to secure a ceasefire, provide humanitarian assistance, and superintend the evacuation of ECOWAS citizens and other foreign nationals trapped in Liberia.[23]

Many of the legal, operational and resource weaknesses (and shortcomings) of the ECOMOG intervention in Liberia are well documented.[24] As Pitts[25] has rightly argued: "the assumption of conflict resolution responsibilities by African sub-regional organizations pointed to a new type of interventionism on the African continent". Levitt[26] traced this 'African-solution-to-African-problems' to attempts by African states to reassert themselves as international power brokers in order to obtain or sustain legitimacy and respect in the global order. The variations in the attainment of 'home grown' peace-building initiatives, however, differ considerably as a result of differences in trust building in the pre-intervention period of the conflict. From this line of argument, one of the challenges that faced ECOMOG in Liberia (as against, for instance, its operations in Sierra Leone) related directly to the degree of pre-intervention trust building that either took place or never did at all. According to him, interventionist states

97

must possess four key attributes: legitimacy, resource capacity, sub-regional doctrine formulation and transparency, all of which are important ingredients for "post-intervention operational outcomes and the extent to which a humanitarian enforcement operation may succeed". Undoubtedly, these prerequisites were in acute supply within the West African sub-region at the time ECOWAS contemplated and commenced its operations in Liberia.

Having said this, the fundamental point to add is that the intervention by ECOMOG in Liberia ended the long era of non-interference in the internal affairs of member-states; a principle hitherto held as sacrosanct, and boldly enshrined in the Charter of the Organization of African Unity (OAU) [27]. For ECOWAS, it provided the first instance when the purely sub-regional economic cooperation institution was experimented with such an ambitious peacekeeping project in the face of the unconscionable reluctance by the international community to lend a hand.[28] Even when the international community did, it was certainly a first instance of supporting military intervention by a regional actor in a sovereign state without prior authorization by the United Nations Security Council. Finally, it was the first case involving the simultaneous deployment of a UN Observer Mission, the UNOMIL, and a peace enforcement mission mounted by a sub-regional body in the same country.[29] Despite its evident shortcomings, the ECOMOG-UNOMIL partnership has become a successful example in terms of partnership and responsibility sharing in peacekeeping operations between the UN and a regional agency.

Whatever criticisms that have been leveled against ECOMOG's operations in Liberia (and they are legion!)[30], what none of its critics can deny is that the Force played a pivotal role in ensuring that the civil war did not physically spill beyond the Mano River Union zone. Besides, ECOMOG troops ensured that Monrovia remained a safe haven for those fleeing the highly insecure countryside. Perhaps the casualty rate would have skyrocketed had many of those who sought refuge in the capital stayed back in their towns and villages by the time the rebels struck. Again, ECOMOG was alone until 1993 when the United Nations Security Council (UNSC) approved the establishment of the UN Observer Mission in Liberia (UNOMIL), which was to work in an unprecedented partnership with ECOMOG and the OAU in supervising the transition process.[31] This contrasts sharply with the situation in neighboring Sierra Leone where the post-war reconstruction efforts of the government in Freetown are enjoying the support of friendly governments of the UK and USA, and the international donor community at large.

3.5 Uneasy Peace and Post-War Instability

Even an arm-chair observer of the political landscape in post-war Liberia cannot be fooled into believing that the country would enjoy a durable peace for too long. No doubt, the immediate build-up to the post-war political dispensation was neither conducive for peace and stability nor for the enthronement of enduring democracy in the war torn country. For instance, by February 1997 when ECOWAS announced that voting by proportional representation would take place on May 30 to elect the President and a two-tier legislature, it was indisputable that the major stakeholders, particularly the warring factions, were far from ready to submit themselves for an uncertain electoral process fearing that the outcome may be hijacked by the dominant party, the National Patriotic Party (NPP) led by its warlord, Charles Taylor. Besides all that, it was also obvious that the electorate, even though eagerly looking forward to the restoration of normalcy, was not fully prepared for the polls as many were still nursing physical, emotional, medical and psychological wounds from their bitter war experiences. Not surprisingly, when the result of the election was announced, Taylor secured an outright victory, winning 75.3% of the votes cast; leaving the runner-up, Mrs. Johnson-Sirleaf, with only 9.6%.

Despite Taylor's victory at the polls, the electoral process was evidently fraught with major problems, the most important being widespread allegations of intimidation and harassment of opponents by NPP members.

To this can be added the general concern that the process was actually externally engineered to bring Taylor to power at all cost; since the converse would have led to the continuation of the civil war. Beyond the electoral problems, many observers have also claimed, with some justification, that Taylor has neither transcended the deep animosity of the civil war years nor did he brace himself adequately for the statesmanship role necessary for guiding Liberia peacefully out of the woods. There is sense in the accusation, therefore, that he was still overwhelmed by the warlord mentality that saw him through the civil war years in the bush, and that he has not made the important transition from a warlord to that of a national leader acceptable to other interest groups in his country. In the face of staggering post-war reconstruction problems and challenges, President Taylor has done little to ameliorate the psychological trauma and social plights facing his people. Thus, it is plausible to argue that perhaps the greatest stumbling block to peace and stability in post-war Liberia is the heavy handed and uneven political and administrative style of President Taylor, since he came to power in 1997.

There are obviously daunting problems facing post-war Liberia that the regime of Charles Taylor has either not addressed at all, or only did so half heartedly five years after his ascension to the presidency. One of these is resettling and rehabilitating the huge population displaced as a result of the civil war. By 1997 when the civil war ended, the number of Liberian refugees in different West African countries remained staggering. Out of a total of 667, 000 refugees, neighboring Guinea and Cote d'Ivoire played host to 420, 000 and 210, 000 refugees respectively. Ghana, Nigeria and Sierra Leone each had 17, 000; 6, 000; and 14, 000 refugees.[32] Unfortunately, refugee-related issues do not seem to be a priority of the present government, which is preoccupied more with regime survival and stability than alleviating the desperate economic and social conditions of the vast majority of Liberians. In March 1999, two years after it started the mass repatriation of Liberian refugees, at a cost of 60 million US dollars, the

United Nations High Commission for Refugees (UNHCR) estimated that some 220, 000 refugees and 56, 000 internally displaced Liberians were still on their long waiting list for resettlement and rehabilitation. Even as late as the first quarter of 2002, the Commission continued to voice persistent concerns about the status of Liberian refugees at home and in the Diaspora.

Table 3.1: Refugee Population in West Africa

Country of Domicile	Refugees in Different West African States (1997)		
	Census	Registered	Organized
Guinea	420,000	235, 000	117, 500
Cote d'Ivoire	210, 000	210, 000	105, 000
Ghana	17, 000	15, 000	15, 000
Nigeria	6, 000	6, 000	6, 000
Sierra Leone	14, 000	14, 000	-
Total	667, 000	480, 000	235, 500

Source: UNHCR Country Plan, November 1997[33]

One politico-security repercussion of the poor management of refugee issues is the ease with which they are readily available for use as potent tools for subverting post-war peace-building and reconciliation efforts in the country. Surprisingly, whereas almost all attention is focused on the plight and persecutions of refugees, not much is said about their destabilizing activities. On many occasions, refugees have been known to engage in activities that caused or exacerbated socio-political unrest and upheavals that from time to time threatened both their home country and host State (s). It is impossible to forget, for instance, how Charles Taylor actively sponsored dissident Sierra Leonean refugees within the rank and file of his NPFL to launch an attack on Sierra Leone under the banner of the Revolutionary United Front, (RUF) which started one of the most brutal civil wars in Africa's post independence history.[34] Significantly, also, the new insurgent movement, the Liberians United for Reconstruction and

Democracy (LURD), presently engaged in renewed fighting against the Taylor government is known to draw its supporters from among refugees in Sierra Leone, Guinea and Cote d'Ivoire, among others, as well as Liberians within the country who feel disgruntled and disenfranchised in the post-war state-building enterprise of Charles Taylor. And they are many, for understandable reasons too.

One striking feature of recent civil wars in Africa is the extensive and indiscriminate use of children and minors below the age of 18 years as combatants by warlords: in Somalia, Sudan, Mozambique, Sierra Leone and Liberia.[35] In Liberia, all the major warring factions (including the Armed Forces of Liberia, AFL) actively recruited and armed minors, child soldiers. Unfortunately, diplomatic rhetoric and vain political commitments have not been matched by serious public policy action on the part of the Taylor government towards ameliorating the plight of ex-child soldiers in particular, and ex-combatants in general. In fact, a handful of the ex-child soldiers, or *soya boys*, as they are called in local parlance, have been conscripted into the Special Security Unit detailed to guard President Taylor. They roam the streets in military fatigue with AK-47 assault rifles dangling on their shoulders. Over the years, they have gained notoriety for unruly public conduct and intimidation.

The wartime exploits of child soldiers have attracted a lot of media, academic and international public policy attention. Indiscriminate child soldiering marked the civil war in Liberia (See Chapter Four in this volume for more on the phenomenon in Liberia and neighboring Sierra Leone). The individual and collective memories of their exploits, as well as the public and private opprobrium directed towards them in many communities, cannot be ignored. Many of the ex-child soldiers, according to Human Rights Watch/ Africa, continue to suffer symptoms of post-trauma stress disorder, insomnia, nightmares, anxiety and depression. (See Chapter Five for more on this subject). Perhaps what is important to reiterate is that their long and sustained exposure to living dangerously cannot but have far-reaching implications for post-war peace and stability in Liberia. Their plight is further complicated by the curious decision of the Taylor government not to acknowledge, much less pay attention to their immediate problems. Although Taylor's NPFL was a major culprit in the indiscriminate use of minors as combatants, his government has openly and repeatedly insisted that it does not intend to glorify their exploits over and above those of other categories of combatants and war-affected youths in the country. With the benefit of hindsight, this policy has contributed in no small way to the present state of affairs in the country, which the LURD was able to exploit to advantage.

Many of the children who participated in the war at very tender ages have now grown into young adults. During this period of maturity, they have become very conscious of their social and political statuses, rights and privileges. It is difficult not to notice that the pent-up anger and frustration in them cannot be contained for too long. Many of the ex-combatants are piqued that Taylor's NPFL used and dumped them unfairly. Majority of the child soldiers are out of school, unemployed and are roaming the streets of Monrovia. They have also been implicated in the steeply rising wave of urban and rural crimes in post-war Liberia. Certainly, there is an urgent imperative for the government to reconcile itself with the fact that unrehabilitated, un-reintegrated and unemployed ex-child soldiers and other former combatants are not only a great nuisance, but could also indeed complicate and/or threaten successful post-war stability and reconstruction in the country. Thus one important way forward would be for Taylor's government to emulate and build on the long and successful record of social, economic and psychological interventions by third sector institutions, including community-based non-governmental organizations, church-based groups and international advocacy/ humanitarian agencies in ameliorating the multi-dimensional problems currently facing ex-fighters in Liberia.

Undoubtedly, the civil war in Liberia has hindered the expansion of critical social capital and infrastructure needed for economic and social development, subverted the creation of a stable security architecture, stunted the growth of a vibrant civil society, and heightened the propensity for a self-perpetuating culture of violence, which is difficult to tame. Even at the time of writing, 2003, much of the social infrastructure ravaged by the long civil war was yet to be fully restored. Indeed, the scars of war are still very evident all over the country, most especially in Monrovia, where majority of the Liberian population presently reside. Of course, these are only the visible and tangible signs of the bloody civil war; but there are even more intangible but nonetheless significant problems facing the government of Taylor, including the weakening or total collapse of the family structure, traditional value systems and authority on which societal norms, attitudes, beliefs and institutions are constructed and sustained in the pre-war years.

What makes the Liberian situation of such grave concern is that the government of Charles Taylor continues to pay lip service to these serious problems and challenges facing the country. A popular refrain in official circles in Monrovia is the intention of government to take Liberia out of Monrovia; meaning literally, scaling down or completely ignoring repairs of the social infrastructure in the capital destroyed by Charles Taylor's NPFL forces in 1992 in preference for other parts of the country. On the surface, it can be argued that taking development to the doorsteps of previously excluded folks in the countryside is desirable and timely considering their long years of neglect and exclusion. In reality, however, the policy implies that the time has come for Taylor to punish the elite and more privileged inhabitants of Monrovia who still constitute the bedrock of the opposition to his regime, and who had almost scuttled his way to the Executive Mansion earlier. Perhaps this is one of the reasons why president Taylor has not made any concerted effort to ease the discomfort of the middle class by restoring the municipal services (particularly electricity and water), which his NPFL destroyed during Operation Octopus in 1992. Not surprisingly, living and doing business in the country is now also much more expensive as residents and business operators have to rely on standby generators for electricity. Again, the citizens for long had to rely on the EU whose tankers supply portable drinking water to overhead tanks located strategically in different parts of the city on daily basis.

Aside from this already depressing socio-economic situation in the country, there are the lingering impacts of the halfhearted disarmament of former fighters after the civil war in 1997. Contrary to claims by government agencies, ECOMOG, the rebel factions, and indeed, the provisions of the peace accords, the disarmament programme was both epileptic and therefore inconclusive. Indeed, in March and April 1997, ECOMOG made stunning discoveries of caches of arms and ammunitions at the residence of one of the faction leaders, Alhaji Kromah, in Monrovia and Voinjama, as well as two other sites in the former NPFL strongholds in Nimba County. With some justifications, also, it is plausible to expect that some of the wartime command structures of the various rebel groups were not sufficiently dismantled. This suspicion was confirmed in 1998 when supporters of Roosevelt Johnson rearmed and launched an attack on government positions in Monrovia. Many of the former fighters that were interviewed during fieldwork claimed that rather than turning their weapons in, many of them simply buried them as insurance policy, reasoning that if war were to break out again, they would not be caught with their pants down. Many of the key informants confirmed that the former rebel leaders still commanded obedience and loyalty from rank and file ex-combatants, especially ex-child soldiers who still looked up to them for assistance and protection. Under the circumstances, it is hardly surprising that the rebel LURD movement successfully remobilized and re-launched attacks in different parts of the country aimed both at destabilizing and toppling the authoritarian and rather insensitive government of Charles Taylor in late 2000, thereby starting a second civil war in the already war torn society.

These developments portend grave dangers for postwar peace building and reconstruction in Liberia. Apart from the obvious domestic complications of the present insurgency, there is also some anxiety that the renewed fighting in Liberia could adversely affect the fragile peace that is so far holding in neighbouring Sierra Leone, Guinea and indeed the rest of the sub-region. There is credence to some of these fears because, after all, the eleven-year civil war in Sierra Leone was directly linked to the war in neighboring Liberia.

What all the above suggests, then, is the urgent need for Taylor's government to demonstrate some sincerity of purpose and the political will to embark upon a genuine policy of reconciliation and peace and confidence building in Liberia, so that all stakeholders will be assured that they have a future in the country. Such assurance is imperative for as long as there is widespread perception that Taylor is mortgaging the collective future of Liberians, it would be difficult to stem the tide of opposition to the regime in Monrovia and by implication, the festering rebellion led by the LURD Movement. But can Charles Taylor rise up to the challenge? Can he successfully shed his warlord garb and put on the toga of a statesman? Answers to these questions are bound to change the fortunes of Liberia one-way or the other.

From such a perspective the scenarios for the country are rather bleak. It is arguable that Liberia is at the moment caught between a rock and a hard place. There are accordingly, two broad scenarios. The first scenario is a violent overthrow of Charles Taylor's regime in a coup d'etat by dissidents within his government. This is rather far fetched given the elaborate security fortress he has surrounded himself with. The second scenario is equally unrealistic at least in the short and medium terms; that is a takeover of the State by the rebel LURD Movement. For now at least, it is not possible for the LURD to defeat Taylor on the battlefield. And even if we assume that Taylor were to be overthrown, who will credibly take over from him without a power struggle and even greater bloodshed? The inevitable and gloomy conclusion from all this is that Liberia is in for a prolonged and vicious cycle of strife and socio-economic and political instability. Expectedly, the lot of the ordinary citizen is not an enviable one. The continuing violence and insecurity can only aggravate their already desperate socio-economic plights. The situation is compounded by the continuing pariah status of Charles Taylor in the international community. It is hoped that the international community in conjunction with ECOWAS leaders, would bring enough pressure to bear on Charles Taylor to put in place policies that would heal the wounds of the civil war and provide a congenial environment for genuine post war peace building, reconstruction and reconciliation in Liberia. That is the only viable option in the prevailing circumstances in Liberia. However, if the antecedents of Taylor are anything to go by, such a scenario is also rather overly optimistic. Liberia is therefore in for a rough ride indeed.

Notes and References

1. For more on this phenomenon, see Sesay, A. (1980) "Societal Inequalities Ethnic heterogeneity and Political Instability: The Case of Liberia" in *Plural Societies*, Vol. 11, No. 3, 1980: 15-30; and Nmoma, Veronica (1997), "The Civil War and Refugee Crisis in Liberia", *The Journal of Conflict Studies*, Volume XVII, No. 1, Spring 1997: 101-125

2. Kieh, George Klay Jr. (1988), "Setting the Stage: Historical Antecedents to the April 12, 1980 Coup d'Etat in Liberia", *Liberian Studies Journal*, XIII: 1988

3. Adeleke, Ademola, (1995) "The Politics and Diplomacy of Peacekeeping in West Africa: The ECOWAS Operation in Liberia", *The Journal of Modern African Studies*, 33, 4 (1995): 573ff

4. Janet, Fleishman, (1993),"Uncivil War", *Africa Report*, May-June, 1993

5. William Reno (1998), **Warlord Politics and African States**, Boulder and London: Lynne Rienner Publishers, Ellis, Stephen (1998)), "Liberia's Warlord Insurgency", in Christopher Clapham (ed)(1998), **African Guerrillas**, Oxford: James Currey, Yekutiel Gershoni (1997), "War without end an end to a War: The Prolonged wars in Liberia and Sierra Leone", *African Studies Review,* 40, 3: December: 55-76

6. Alao, A and Olonisakin, F.(2000), "Economic Fragility and political fluidity: Explaining Natural Resources and Conflict", in *International peacekeeping,* Vol.7, No. 4, winter, 29.

7. Reno, William (1996), "The Business of War in Liberia" *Current History,* 95: Paul Richards (1996), "The Sierra Leone-Liberia Boundary Wilderness: Rain Forests, Diamonds and War", in Paul Nugent and A.I. Asiwaju (eds.)(1996), **African Boundaries: Barriers, Conduits and Opportunities**, London: Pinter, and O'Neill, William (1993), "Liberia: An avoidable Tragedy", *Current History,* 92: 1993

8. Dusty Wolokorie, Figures cited in **Report on the Survey of Prospects for Micro-Financing Activities in Lofa County,** prepared by Third World Consultancy Inc. of Liberia for Doan Foundation of the Netherlands, 1998.

9. Stephen, Ellis (1999), **The Mask of Anarchy: The Destruction of Liberia and the Religious Dimension of an African Civil War,** London: Hurst and Company.

10. It later turned out that ECOMOG had over-inflated that figure, for by January 1997, the national disarmament and demobilization commission claimed 23, 416 disarmed soldiers. The deadline for disarmament was later extended by one week, and in the end, ECOMOG claimed that 91% of forces had been processed.

11. Moose, George E (1996), "Pursuing Peace in Liberia", US Department of State Dispatch, 7 (20), May 13, 244-245

12. See "Peace Process at Standstill Despite Accra Agreement", UN Chronicle, XXXII (3), September 1995: 20; also "Peace Agreement Concluded", UN Chronicle, XXXII (1), March 1995: 26-27

13. At the time of concluding this chapter, Cote d'Ivoire - once celebrated as an "oasis of stability" in West Africa - had imploded into another catastrophic civil war. Already, several properties and lives have been lost, including that of the former Head of State, General Robert Guei. The insurgents have threatened to unleash an unprecedented maelstrom of bloodletting if their grievances are not attended to with dispatch.

14. Regardless of the outcomes of the Abuja meeting, it is important to recall that it facilitated a one-on-one 'reconciliatory' meeting between Charles Taylor and the Nigerian leader, General Sani Abacha.

15. Adisa, Jinmi (1993), "Nigeria in ECOMOG: Political Undercurrents and the Burden of Community Spirit", Jide Owoeye (1993)(ed.), **Nigeria in International Institutions,** Ibadan: College Press Limited, andMortimer, Robert A (1996), "Senegal's Role in ECOMOG: The Francophone Dimension in the Liberian Crisis", JMAS, 34. 2 (1996): 293-306

16. Levitt, Jeremy (1999), "Pre-Intervention Trust-Building, African States and Enforcing the Peace: The Case of ECOWAS in Liberia and Sierra Leone", *Liberian Studies Journal,* XXIV, 1 (1999): 1-26

17. Yekutiel Gershoni (1997), "Military and Diplomatic Strategies in the Liberian Civil War", *Liberian Studies Journal,* XXII (2), 1997: 199-239; Conteh-Morgan, Earl (1998), "Conflict and Regional Peacekeeping: ECOMOG's Hegemonic Role in Liberia and Sierra Leone", *Liberian Studies Journal,* XXIII, 2 (1998): 78-92

18. Mackinlay, J and Alao, A (1995), **Liberia 1994: ECOMOG and UNOMIL Response to a Special Emergency,** UN University, Occasional paper No.1

19. Aning, Emmanuel Kwesi (1996), "Ghana, ECOWAS and the Liberian Crisis: An Analysis of Ghana's Role in Liberia", *Liberian Studies Journal,* XXI, 2 (1996): 259-299

20. Nwolise, O.B.C (1993), "The Diplomacy of Peace-Keeping", in M.A. Vogt and A.E. Ekoko (eds.), **Nigeria in International Peace-Keeping**, Lagos: Malthouse, 1993, 293-314

21. ECOMOG was a product of the realities and exegeses that marked the outbreak (and unique circumstances) of the Liberian civil war juncture. Much like the blue Helmet- the United Nations Peacekeeping Force- ECOMOG is not explicitly provided for in the Treaty establishing the Economic Community of West African States (ECOWAS). See Iweze,, C.Y., "Nigeria in Liberia: The Military Operations of ECOMOG", in M.A. Vogt and E.E. Ekoko (eds)(1993), **Nigeria in International Peace-keeping, 1960-1992.** Lagos: Malthouse Press Limited.

22. Kuffor, Kofi Oteng (1993), "The Legality of the Intervention in the Liberian Civil War by the Economic Community of West African States", *African Journal of International and Comparative Law,* 5, 3: 1993: 525-560;

23. For more on this, see Sesay, A (200), "West African military interventions in the 1990s: The Case of ECOWAS in Liberia and Sierra Leone", in L. Du Plessis and M. Hough (eds.), **Managing African Conflicts; the Challenge of Military Intervention**, Pretoria: Human Sciences Research Council/CEMIS and ISSUP

24. Pitts, Michelle (1999), "Sub-Regional Solutions for African Conflict: The ECOMOG Experience", *The Journal of Conflict Studies,* Volume XIX, No. 1, Spring 1999: 51; Van Walraven, Klaas (1999), **The Pretense of Peacekeeping: ECOMOG, West Africa and Liberia (1990-1998)**. Netherlands Institute of International Relations (Clingendael), November 1999; Herbert Howe (1997), "Lessons of Liberia: ECOMOG and Regional Peacekeeping", *International Security,* 21, 3: 1997

25. Levitt, Op. Cit., 1

26. See, in particular, Article III (2) (3) of the OAU Charter for details on the principle of non-interference in the internal affairs of member-states.

27. Adeleke, Op. Cit., p. 569
28. The 300-strong personnel of the United Nations Observer Mission in Liberia (UNOMIL) was established by Security Council Resolution 866 of September 1993 to implement the Cotonou Agreement already endorsed by Interim Government of National Unity (IGNU), ULIMO and the NPFL. See UN Chronicle, XXXII (1) March 1995: 27)
29. One of the most fundamental of the criticisms was that the genesis and genealogy of ECOMOG makes it far from neutral and impartial. Hence, it was not just suspected by Cote d'Ivoire and Burkina Faso, but also by the major rebel factions engaged in the civil war. Throughout the civil war, and after, Taylor's NPFL harbored the deepest suspicion of Nigeria/ ECOMOG. See Levitt, 1999; op. cit, Iweze, 1993, op. cit. For a useful insight into the operational challenges faced by ECOMOG in the Liberian operation, see C. Iweze in Vogt and Ekoko (eds.)(1993); and Adibe, Clement E (1997), "The Liberian Conflict and the ECOWAS-UN Partnership", *Third World Quarterly*, 18, 3: 1997
30. Although a drastically reduced UNOMIL stayed back to oversee the first post-war General Election and the inauguration of Taylor's presidency, it was dissolved in September 1997, just before the enormous tasks of post-war reconstruction were about to commence.
31. See Veronica Nnoma (1999), "The Civil War and the Refugee Crisis in Liberia", *Journal of Conflict Studies*, XVII: 1, Spring 1999: 101-125; M. Elizabeth Smit(2000), "Children War Games", in *Conflict Trends*, 1/2000: 12-17, The African Centre for the Constructive Resolution of Disputes (ACCORD), South Africa; Ilene Cohn and Guy S. Godwin-gill (1994), "Child Soldiers: The Role of Children in Armed Conflicts", Oxford: Clarendon Press, 1994
32. Wolokorie, Op. Cit., 13
33. The extent of NPFL support- resource, logistic, personnel and operational- to the Revolutionary United Front (RUF) main bases in

southern Kailahun District has been well documented in Paul Richards (1996), "The Sierra Leone-Liberian Boundary Wilderness".

34. Groves, Dennis (2000), **Rebuilding the Future: Child Soldiers and Sustainable Disarmament**, Centre for Defense Information (Monograph Series), April 2000: 1-35

35. Furley, Oliver (1995), "Child Soldiers in Africa", in Oliver Furley (ed.)(1995), **Conflict in Africa**, London: Tauris Publishers; Human Right Watch/ Africa (1994), **Easy Prey: Child Soldiers in Liberia,** Human Rights Watch/ Africa. New York: HRW; Groves, Dennis,(2000) **Rebuilding the Future: Child Soldiers and Sustainable Disarmament,** Centre for Defense Information (Monograph Series), April 2000: 1-35

Chapter Four: Sierra Leone: The Long Descent into Civil War

Charles Ukeje

4.1 Introduction

On 23 March 1991, a band of armed men led by a hitherto unknown former army Corporal, Foday Sankoh, under the umbrella of the Revolutionary United Front, RUF, launched a blistering cross-border attack from neighboring Liberia in Kailahun District. That invasion, initially interpreted by the government in Freetown, the capital of Sierra Leone, as a minor skirmish between smugglers and border patrol police, soon blossomed into a full-scale civil war that would haunt and traumatize the small West African state for about a decade.[1] In many ways, the insurgency against Sierra Leone was a by-product of the Liberian civil war. The RUF that launched the invasion was known to have received more than mere casual endorsement from Charles Taylor, the Liberian warlord, who had launched his own insurgency a year and half earlier in December 1989 with the ambition of toppling the corrupt and vindictive regime of Samuel Kanyon Doe.

It is clear that apart from fighting alongside the National Patriotic Front of Liberia (NPFL), the RUF was largely funded, armed and encouraged by Taylor to attack Sierra Leone. By instigating the invasion of Sierra Leone, Taylor's intentions for supporting the RUF were two-fold: in the first instance, he had his eyes on the rich diamond deposits in the part of Sierra Leone adjoining Liberia to fund his own insurgency (and hopefully, his junta);[2] and second, he had the intention of punishing the government of President Saidu Momoh for allowing Sierra Leone to be used as a staging post not only by anti NPFL fighters, but for actually contributing to the multinational peace-keeping force, the ECOWAS Monitoring Group's (ECOMOG) intervention in Liberia. It was shortly after the onset of the

113

ECOMOG intervention in Liberia that Taylor openly threatened to launch an attack on Sierra Leone's Lungi airport, ECOMOG's operational base, in order to teach Sierra Leone an unforgettable lesson.[3]

Regardless of that however, the role of external forces, particularly those of Taylor and Liberia, only gives a partial, incomplete explanation of the genesis and trajectory of the civil war in Sierra Leone. The remote and underlying causes are buried much deeper in the socio-political structures of the Sierra Leonean state itself dating back into the colonial days and after independence, when the departing British rulers handed over power to a group of local elites. As in many other British colonies in Africa, attempt was made to hand over the reins of power only to pliable and acquiescent local elites who cooperated with colonial rule. It was therefore in conformity with that tradition that power was handed over to Dr. Milton Margai of the Sierra Leone Peoples Party (SLPP) as the first Prime Minister upon the country's formal independence in 1961. He was to be succeeded in 1964 by his half-brother Dr. Albert Margai.[4] The rule of the SLPP ended in 1968 when Dr. Siaka Stevens of the All Peoples Congress (APC) became the Prime Minister, thus setting off two decades of corruption, misrule and authoritarianism. Effective from 1978, the constitution was modified to make the APC the only legal party in the country, thus paving way for over-centralization of power and one-party rule, with its attendant contractions. One of the enduring legacies of the protracted misrule by the APC, especially as it related to the outbreak of the civil war in 1991, was the groundswell of an army of unemployed, *lumpenised* youths from whose ranks the RUF guerrillas were initially recruited.[5]

Perhaps if the government in Freetown had correctly perceived the March 1991 trans-–border invasion as a serious enough threat to national security and even its own survival, its response might have been totally different and more decisive. As the insurgency progressed, the government in Freetown shifted from labeling it a clash between smugglers and border patrols to that of disgruntled elements supported by Charles Taylor's guerrillas. The government of President Saidu Momoh was to pay the price for its naivety when a year later, in April 1992, a group of actually disgruntled military officers fresh from the battlefield in the war against the RUF overthrew his corrupt and inept government.[6] Their major grouse with President Momoh was that the government in Freetown was not handling the war well, as it failed to adequately equip the Sierra Leone Armed forces to repel the invasion, and that soldier's welfare was sacrificed with reckless abandon. The leader of the mutinous soldiers, Captain Valentine Strasser, formed a new junta, the National Provisional Ruling Council (NPRC), which promptly made clear its intention to, amongst other things, end the civil war. While this resolve dovetailed with the yearnings of the armed forces, it was also "good riddance" to the bad, corrupt and ethnically centred government of the APC.

Unfortunately, while the regime of Momoh could not terminate the invasion, the successor junta led by Strasser never achieved success in de-escalating or terminating it either. This was probably responsible for turning what was, *ab initio,* a mere cross-border incursion by a rag-tag guerrilla force, into a bloody civil war that would last for a decade before peace was imposed by ECOMOG, the UN, and Britain. The popularly elected civilian regime of President Ahmed Tejan Kabbah was bedeviled by the almost intractable civil war during its first five years in office.

4.2 Internationalizing the Civil War

Unable to effectively and unilaterally contain the cross-border invasions by Foday Sankoh's RUF and its Liberian supporters, the Sierra Leonean government unwittingly internationalized the civil war with the involvement of Nigerian and Guinean troops. But it must also be stated that the war had an international flavour right from the beginning. This was because of the inspiration, financial, military and logistics support from Charles Taylor's National Patriotic Front of Liberia (NPFL), the clandestine involvement of Libya, which provided initial training and funding for the RUF guerrillas, and Burkina Faso, which supplied mercenaries. In addition, the initial RUF

115

invasion force had in its ranks nationals from several West African countries who were mercenaries. But it was the overt intervention of two sub-regional states, Nigeria and Guinea that was deemed as the most crucial turning point in the war.

The intervention of these West African countries was probably inevitable, given both the inability of the Sierra Leonean army to contain the insurgency as well as the presence of foreign troops on Sierra Leonean soil prior to the crisis. In the first instance, the support of the Guinean troops was invoked on the strength of a subsisting bilateral defence agreement between the two contiguous neighbours. The troops were promptly deployed to bolster the Sierra Leonean forces. The involvement of Nigerian troops on the other hand, was rather fortuitous. It was not in response to any such bilateral agreement, but the presence of troops from that country in Sierra Leone as part of the ECOMOG contingent to Liberia. They were part of the defence of the rear base of the ECOMOG troops stationed in Sierra Leone.[7]

Nigeria's own involvement is also better appreciated within the context of the long-standing and cordial bilateral relations between the two former British colonies, and much more so in the unflinching support that Sierra Leonean president, Saidu Momoh, gave to the ECOMOG venture in Liberia. It would be recalled that the entire ECOMOG idea, from conception to implementation, was the brainchild of Nigeria's then military ruler, General Ibrahim Babangida.[8] It was his suggestion that an ECOWAS Standing Mediation Committee (ESMC) be established to monitor developments in the sub-region and make recommendations to the ECOWAS Authority for nipping conflicts in the bud. It was this ESMC that later took the decision to send a peacekeeping force to Liberia in August 1990.[9] The conception of a sub-regional military force to intervene in the Liberian crisis for humanitarian and other considerations received full endorsement and encouragement from the Sierra Leonean government. It was the *sine qua non* for the launching of the ECOMOG operation since the consent and support of the contiguous neighbour was considered strategic. Sierra Leone also contributed a contingent of soldiers to the multinational intervention force and allowed the use of its territory as a staging post for troop and material deployment into Liberia. A contingent of Nigeria's own forces was thus retained in Sierra Leone to provide protection for ECOMOG's intervention force. It was a detachment of this force that was promptly deployed alongside the Sierra Leonean forces to bolster the country's defence during the course of the civil war.

The Nigerian involvement was probably predictable not only on the strength of long-standing bilateral relations alone, but more importantly as already noted, because of the perception that a country that was doing so much for the multilateral intervention in Liberia must not be allowed to suffer the adverse consequences of that support. It would be recalled that the authorities in Freetown did not withdraw their contingent from ECOMOG in spite of the precarious national security situation at home. This steadfast support for the ECOMOG joint venture, more than any other factor, was responsible for Nigeria's active defence of the country. Besides, it must be understood that once Taylor had threatened to teach that country a lesson for its participation in the sub-regional intervention, Sierra Leone deserved every support it could get especially from Nigeria, the acknowledged powerhouse behind ECOMOG.

It would have been morally unsustainable for that country to be left to stew in its own juice on account of the peacekeeping operations in Liberia. The truth is that if Sierra Leone had withdrawn its forces from ECOMOG to face the situation at home, the fragile credibility of the entire ECOMOG peacekeeping mission to Liberia would have been severely dented, especially against the background of the hostile position taken by a number of francophone states in the sub-region that were openly skeptical about the Anglophone preponderance among the troop-contributing states. They were not supportive of the operation, especially after Charles Taylor had derided the ECOMOG force as Nigeria's Trojan horse for the colonization of Liberia and the domination of the sub-region of West Africa. Nigeria's support for the Sierra Leone Armed Forces, however, continued even after Captain Valentine Strasser overthrew President Momoh, as Abuja gave considerable artillery support as a reward for the retention of his contingent in the Liberia operation in spite of the civil war at home.[10] The same support was extended to all the country's subsequent governments, including that of President Ahmed Tejan Kabbah much later until the formal end of the war in early 2002.

4.3 The Unwholesome Character of the Civil War

Unlike many other similar intra-state conflicts in Africa that are unique by their ethnic coloration, the civil war in Sierra Leone was devoid of any such classification. It had neither ethnic, regional, religious, nor a sectarian coloration. In addition, it was not a Cold War-induced civil war. In fact, it is better classified by its patent lack of well-defined and clearly articulated political objectives, even though it initially appeared directed at overthrowing the ignoble APC government of Saidu Momoh. While seizing power might have been part of the vaguely defined objectives of the insurgency, it was never really articulated in any concrete way that would have helped the RUF to mobilize public support. Aside from the fact that the initial leadership of the RUF received some military training in Libya, the group had no ethnic agenda, ideological purpose or direction. As Ibrahim Abdullah observes, the RUF was neither a revolutionary organization (the revolution in its name notwithstanding) nor a liberation movement properly speaking, since all it did was to perpetrate unspeakable atrocities against civilian populations.[11] It lacked organization and discipline, and its leaders and other ranks behaved exactly like the common bandits that they really were. Not being a proper revolutionary organization or liberation movement, the RUF was lacking in ideological direction, it was not dependent on any outside power for assistance and weapons, as its weapons were sourced

118

from illicit private arms merchants and paid for by pillaging the country's diamonds and timber. This leads one to conclude, as Paul Richards has done in his highly controversial study **Fighting for the Rain Forest, that** the initiators of the violence that metamorphosed into a bloody civil war can be "better pictured as criminals and bandits."[12]

In a more profound sense, the civil war in Sierra Leone was characterized by extreme brutality. The RUF operations were notable for the extreme savagery and brutality they unleashed upon innocent and defenseless civilian population, and by looting, burning of villages and settlements, hostage-taking, abduction of young children to elicit cooperation and for their use as child soldiers, wanton rape and deliberate amputation of the limbs of their victims. Lacking in defined or explicit political objectives, the RUF could not put in place any structures for the administration of even the areas under its control, but instead its members engaged in plunder and banditry as a way of life. Again, the RUF actions were further characterized by the deliberate targeting of civilian population rather than government soldiers or government installations for attacks. More often than not, the RUF fighters scrupulously avoided government soldiers so as to concentrate on their main objective, pillage. This readily debunks whatever revolutionary pretensions the RUF might have had about liberating the people from the clutches of a bad government. And that seems to explain why the guerrilla outfit never really mobilized the people's support.

4.4 The Intractable Civil War

The inability of the government of President Momoh to bring the initial guerrilla invasion of the territory under control or even to quick termination was engendered by a number of critical factors. The small size of the Sierra Leonean army at the initial stages of the war did not help matters, more so since a contingent of the force was already deployed for multilateral operations in Liberia. This situation left the army too thin on the ground to mount effective national defence and repel the externally sponsored

119

invasion. The regime's initial response was to commence large-scale mass recruitment of new soldiers to beef up the force. This rapidly increased the strength of the army from its initial 3,000 officers and men to about 14,000. Most of the new recruits, expectedly, were from the ranks of the lumpen-proletariat and were ill trained. The latter factor was to severely dilute military professionalism and the efficiency of the army as a fighting force.[13]

The woes of the army were further compounded by the lack of modern sophisticated weapons and logistics to effectively respond to the dire situation at hand. Apart from the low rating of the national economy, the stupendous level of official corruption could not allow the ruling APC government of Momoh to acquire the needed hardware and logistics support. The army was thus unable to effectively contain or confront the RUF. This, as we observed earlier, was responsible for the overthrow of the Momoh government. Even then, the succeeding military regime could not do much. Made up of very young and politically inexperienced soldiers (Strasser himself being only 27 years old), the official corruption that wrecked the previous regime merely continued on a grander scale. "State robbery", looting and outright lawlessness became veritable instruments of governance and battle-tested officers who could have commanded the military campaigns at the war front stayed back in the capital for the sheer sybaritic indulgences that government positions and patronages offered.

The attraction provided by vital national resources, especially diamond and timber, further complicated the matter. Since Taylor's main intention for aiding the RUF insurgents in the first place, was to get access to the diamond mines, the RUF was determined to strangulate the country by seizing, controlling and recklessly plundering the diamond deposits. The officers and other ranks of the Sierra Leonean army, mostly ill-trained, poorly paid and under-equipped, also diverted their own attention to illicit mining of diamonds for self-aggrandizement. The army was reputedly more interested in lining the pockets of the officers and men than fighting the rebels. As the invading rebels and disgruntled regular soldiers began nurturing similar objectives and plans, the line separating the soldiers from the rebels thinned out. Both sides engaged in illicit diamond mining, logging and smuggling.[14] Thus soldiers perpetrated the same horrendous atrocities on the civilian populations in the logging and diamond mining districts as the rebels did. When civilians could no longer distinguish between soldiers and rebels, they coined the term "sobels" to refer to soldiers who had become and were behaving exactly like rebels.[15] The complicity between rebels and soldiers did not allow any progress to be made in resolving the civil war. In any case, it was also apparent that the military government in Freetown was not particularly interested in its quick resolution because its own officials were neck deep in corrupt practices; and were thus more than willing to allow the poorly paid and badly equipped soldiers in the war front the latitude to help themselves to state resources.[16] Thus driven by the privatization of natural resources, the civil war continued to fester until it went out of control.

One significant development from the 'sobelisation' of the national army was the emergence of the Kamajor militia group, a civil defence force made up of local hunters and other local volunteers armed with crude weapons and locally fabricated guns, who took on the duty of defending the local communities from the rampaging soldiers and rebel forces. At a point in the civil war, even the government in Freetown enlisted their support against the RUF guerrillas who were threatening the national capital itself. They formed a sort of bulwark against the guerrillas' hit and run raids, ambushes, abductions, hostage taking, maiming of innocent civilians and other sabotage operations as the already severely compromised army could no longer contain the spreading attacks of the RUF. In many cases, the fight often became a tripartite one between the rebels, the soldiers (i.e. the sobels) and the Kamajors.

The international involvement also created additional complications. Nigeria, Ghana, Guinea, Liberia's NPFL, Libya, Burkina Faso, were involved, some surreptitiously while others overtly. With the support of the Guinean, Ghanaian and Nigerian troops, successive governments in Freetown were unwilling to concede grounds to the rebels; neither were they willing to seek any peaceful political resolution as long as Freetown, the capital, was securely policed and protected by the ECOMOG soldiers. While the war was going on badly for government forces, successive governments in Freetown did not see the need for compromise with the rebels, and this made an early political resolution of the war difficult to achieve. This was particularly so since no troop contributing state in the ECOMOG adventure would tolerate any concessions to Charles Taylor and the RUF, which he sponsored and supported. There was an added dimension in that Nigeria, especially, was very uncomfortable with not only Charles Taylor's support for the RUF, but also more importantly, Libya's clandestine support for the rebels. General Babangida of Nigeria made this point very clear when he said that the West African leaders could not stomach any intruder from outside the sub-region to just walk in and take over.[17] This was in addition to the fact that the rebels were trained in Libya and that Burkina Faso actually donated mercenaries to assist them. No easy solution to the war could be found, also because of the multi-dimensional nature of external involvement.

The government of Sierra Leone tacitly accepted its own helplessness and military failure in resolving the invasion when in mid-1995 it hired *Executive Outcomes*, the South African based private mercenary outfit, to bolster its forces on the battlefield. While this mercenary outfit initially proved effective, it later became a prominent liability not only on the battlefield but also as a drain on the nation's lean purse. The mercenaries probably helped in prolonging the war because of their juicy monthly pay of $1.5 million,[18] by a poor country whose army could have benefited greatly had such huge money been expended on equipping it.

A decidedly novel dimension and complication was added to the intractable civil war when in May 1997, the popularly elected civilian government of Ahmed Tejan Kabbah was overthrown by a group of soldiers led by a youthful army major, Johnny Paul Koroma. This new group of putschists was also allied with the rebel forces of the Revolutionary United Front whose own invasion started the civil war in 1991. Lacking in legitimacy because of the popular aversion of the masses in the country to another round of military rule, the new military junta sought to rule the country more by force than by the consent of the people. In an unprecedented mass revolt and civil disobedience, the ordinary people brought government to a standstill as civil servants, teachers and other workers withdrew their services and refused to return to work in spite of entreaties by the new government and threats of deprivation. Even private and informal sector operators scaled or closed down their businesses in the unprecedented campaign of civil disobedience. Unable to govern, both the military junta and its RUF allies engaged in perhaps the most despicable acts of lawlessness and brigandry, while ordinary soldiers embarked on a looting spree. Under the circumstances, the soldiers of the national army and their erstwhile enemies, the RUF, had become one and the same, arrayed against the interests and wishes of the people. That transformation completed what has been referred to as the "sobelisation" of the army.

But the marriage of convenience between the junta and the RUF was not destined to endure for longer than a few weeks, especially as the ambitions of the RUF and its own mission were not necessarily congruent with those of their junta allies. Strains soon developed, as the RUF was unable to achieve its own total objective, just as the junta was unwilling to concede much power to them. The open split between the allies was also inevitable because of the virulent global opposition to the descent to full-blown praetorian rule. The ECOWAS and the OAU refused to accord any recognition to the junta; but instead, continued to regard Kabbah's

123

ousted government as the legitimate government of Sierra Leone. The OAU actually gave open endorsement to ECOWAS and the neighboring states to sniff life out of the Koroma junta by any and all means available to them.[19] The rest of the world outside Africa did not also provide any succour to the regime. The Commonwealth suspended Sierra Leone from membership, while the EU and other regions strongly condemned military rule in the country.

The total isolation of the regime was not only because of the collective domestic and external aversion to military rule alone, but also because of the junta's romance with a guerrilla organization that had deliberately targeted and perpetrated the most barbaric and unspeakable atrocities against an innocent and defenseless civilian population. The RUF's unenviable record was enough consideration to deny the junta any recognition. Stifled by massive civil disobedience at home and completely isolated by the international community, the junta resorted to the brutal tactics of their RUF allies until it was removed from power later in February 1998 by a military invasion of Sierra Leone ordered by General Sani Abacha of Nigeria who was then ECOWAS chairman.

The military campaign mounted by ECOMOG under Nigeria's leadership succeeded in achieving the limited objective of removing Koroma, driving both the junta's forces and its RUF allies into the countryside. In the process, the Sierra Leonean army totally disintegrated and became "sobelised" as large numbers of the soldiers removed their uniforms and joined the rampaging rebel forces of the RUF in their attacks against civilian settlements, pillage and mayhem. The now restored civilian government of President Ahmed Tejan Kabbah remained fragile and at the mercy of the ECOMOG force that provided protection and security in the capital. It was under this rather inauspicious situation that the weak and fragile government in Freetown had to negotiate and conclude a peace agreement with the RUF and remnants of the Koroma junta that had fused with it. The peace agreement brokered by the ECOWAS soon collapsed and hostility once again resumed. It was the intervention of the United Nations and unilateral actions by British forces much later, that began the process that eventually led to the final peace agreement that ended the war in early 2002 as already noted. The United Nations came into the picture with the gradual deployment from November 1999, of the United Nations Mission in Sierra Leone (UNAMSIL) initially commanded by an Indian army officer, Major General Vijay Jetley. While the UNAMSIL was deploying, the British government also sent a contingent of Special Forces to assist the Sierra Leonean government. This force bloodied the rebels by facilitating the arrest of Foday Sankoh and clipping the wings of another fringe group called the West Side Boys.

4.5 The Tortuous Road to Peace

The failure of definitive resolution of the civil war on the battlefield later prompted successive governments in Freetown to attempt the peaceful option. In this case, the governments sought to reach accommodation with the rebels through a series of negotiations and peace accords, many of which broke down and allowed for hostilities to resume in earnest. Apart from a series of negotiated cease-fires that never endured for any length of time because of the insincerity of the rebels themselves, two separate peace agreements were sponsored, negotiated and supervised by the sub-regional body, ECOWAS, and tacitly supported by the global community. The first of such agreements was the Abidjan Peace Accord reached between the government and the RUF on November 30, 1996.[20] The second major one was the July 1999 Lome Agreement negotiated under the auspices of the ECOWAS with support from the UK and US governments.[21] These major sub-regional peace-making efforts were, of course, predated by a number of minor intra-country attempts that never accomplished much.

The Abidjan Peace Accord prescribed, amongst others, the cessation of hostilities by both the government and the rebel forces, for the return of peace; establishment of a national body to be called Commission for the

125

Consolidation of Peace; disarmament, demobilization and reintegration of former combatants; the international monitoring of the encampment, disarmament, demobilization and reintegration process; withdrawal of *Executive Outcomes*, the mercenary outfit engaged by the government; turning the RUF into a political movement with all the rights, privileges and duties under the law; blanket amnesty from prosecution for all RUF members in spite of the atrocities they had committed, etc. The OAU, UNO, Commonwealth and the government of Cote d' Ivoire were nominated as 'moral guarantors' overseeing the faithful implementation of the agreement.[22]

It would appear that the agreement was destined for the trash bin from the onset. While the government was eager for peace and thus negotiated in good faith, the RUF had a different agenda. The government's eagerness to reach a peaceful solution was evident in the concessions granted to the rebels, for example, immunity from prosecution for war crimes and gross human rights violations. The rebels on the other hand, were not sincere about commitment to the dictates of the peace accord. And because the government of the day was too powerless to make significant gains on the battlefield, the RUF was eager to exploit its opponent's weaknesses to subvert the agreement. As a consequence of the lumpen background of its leadership and followers, the RUF was so irredeemably criminal in orientation that it could not meaningfully adapt to normal rules of war. The agreement was thus bound to be short-lived because the democratically elected civilian government of President Tejan Kabbah was overthrown in another putsch on May 25, 1997, as already pointed out in this chapter.

Overall, the Abidjan peace accord could not endure because the RUF was unwilling to forsake its objective of grabbing total power and also because its leadership, profoundly deficient in both intellect and ideology, found it difficult to be part of a regular administration even when they were integrated into it. Besides, it would appear that the RUF was never sincere in any of the negotiations and the resulting peace accords. Its leaders and followers were always fixated on only one objective i.e. to continue their plunder of the diamond mines and other natural resources for private aggrandizement.

In a similar way, it was the depredation of the RUF and its leadership that equally subverted the second major peace agreement signed in Lome. Thus the Lomé Peace Agreement signed with fanfare in July 1999 and witnessed by some of the most prominent West African plenipotentiaries, soon foundered less than a month after it was signed. The agreement was overly optimistic that peace would return once the RUF was pardoned for its horrendous crimes against innocent and defenseless civilians, and integrated into government. Perhaps those who cobbled the agreement together were too naïve to realize that the RUF should not have been trusted to honour its own part of the Agreement. In a manner similar to the defunct Abidjan Peace Accord, the Lome Agreement sought to condone and even compensate the RUF's impunity to commit unspeakable atrocities against civilians. But more profoundly than the Abidjan Accord did, the Lome Agreement not only integrated the RUF into government but actually gave Foday Sankoh a powerful and strategic position that put him in absolute control of the nation's mineral resources, which in a way, also robbed the legitimate government of access to vital economic and financial resources.[23] Thus hobbled by lack of economic power and military might (after the total disintegration of the national army), the government of Kabbah was unwittingly put at the mercy of the RUF, which relentlessly harassed it.

The initial failure of that agreement can be located, amongst other factors, in the unwillingness of the ECOMOG troop contributing states to continue with a virtually un-winnable war that had gulped substantial financial, material and human resources over the years; the complicity of the peacekeeping troops with the rebel forces in the resource plunder that helped to prolong the war; as well as the cynicism of an international community that abandoned Sierra Leone in the hands of West African leaders alone who were increasingly becoming war weary.[24] But then the agreement, both in its negotiation and content, was fatally flawed in other significant regards, which also ensured its quick demise.[25] In a haste to conclude the agreement, the sponsors and guarantors of the peace process decided to overlook the horrendous atrocities committed by the RUF against civilians and even rewarded the guerrillas with juicy government appointments to the bargain. Since impunity to commit crimes against civilians was not punished, the RUF felt obliged to continue in its characteristic lawlessness and thus to subvert the agreement. Jimmy Kandeh's observation perhaps captures it better: "how an agreement that rewards those responsible for some of the worse atrocities committed against civilians in recent memory can be expected to form the basis of 'everlasting peace' is unfathomable."[26] Even though the agreement made provisions for disarming the rebels, it could not be implemented largely because the balance of forces on ground was in RUF's favour. Without a national army under his control, President Tejan Kabbah was hostage to the dictates of ECOMOG and the troop-contributing states and thus rendered powerless to negotiate with the RUF from a vantage position of strength. Besides, the hasty nature of the peace process ignored the vital factor of an existing ceasefire as a *sine qua non* for the implementation of the peace accord. The RUF forces controlled most of the countryside that contains the vital mineral resources and thus its troops could not be demobilized. Having already valorized violence and plunder, the RUF guerrillas were unable to countenance life without terror and looting.

That was the situation until the United Nations Peacekeeping Force began deploying in November 1999 in accordance with the provisions of the Lome peace agreement. The United Nations Mission in Sierra Leone (UNAMSIL) is the largest UN peacekeeping force ever deployed in any country. The large deployment, done piecemeal, and under command of an Indian army General, Vijay Jetley, did not begin to accomplish the restoration of peace until much later.[27] In the first instance, the ECOMOG

Force, which the RUF had hated and wanted out of Sierra Leone, was not withdrawn but integrated into the UNAMSIL. Made up mostly of Nigerian troops, the force did not enjoy the confidence of the RUF and the remnants of the Sierra Leonean armed forces.

Secondly, there was considerable friction between the UNAMSIL commander and Nigerian generals who felt by-passed by the appointment of an Indian to command the UN force in a country in which they and their country had made enormous sacrifices for almost a decade. Consequently, the Indian commander had to report his frustration with the Nigerian officers to the UN Secretary General in a secret memo in which he also accused them of complicity with the RUF in the plunder of the diamond resources. According to General Jetley, his assignment was made all the more difficult because of the collusion of Nigerian officers and the rebels. He specifically mentioned Brigadier-General Maxwell Khobe the ECOMOG Task Force Commander that routed the Koroma junta in Freetown in February 1998, and Major General Gabriel Kpamber, ECOMOG Force Commander, as the two most prominent culprits in the alleged collusion with the rebels for illegal diamond mining and the eventual frustration of the UNAMSIL assignment to restore peace in Sierra Leone. He cited ECOMOG's unwillingness to deploy in certain areas held by the RUF because of the existence of "a tacit understanding... between the RUF and ECOMOG of non-interference in each other's activities..."[28] But all these were in addition to a host of logistics, communications and sundry problems listed in the memo to the Secretary General.

The third factor that initially hindered the restoration of peace after UNAMSIL deployment was, of course, the RUF characteristic insincerity in reaching agreements that they would neither obey nor implement. The RUF was willing to frustrate any international peacekeeping and peace making efforts so long as they held on to the rich diamond mines and other mineral rich areas of the countryside. Every effort by UNAMSIL to deploy in areas held by the RUF was stoutly resisted. Not much could be accomplished also because the troop contributing states were only willing to allow minimal casualties and thus would not allow their soldiers to be deployed to confront RUF resistance.

The deployment of Special Forces by the British government in the second half of 2000 significantly changed the equation. The troops were not part of the UNAMSIL but deployed as part of a bilateral assistance programme to the government of Sierra Leone to train a new national army. Being outside UN command, they were not subjected to the strictures under which UNAMSIL had to operate, and thus were able to launch a bloody commando rescue operation when five of their soldiers were captured and held hostage by a renegade group called the West Side Boys in August 2000. The Special Force also played a major role in the capture of Foday Sankoh later that year, an action that underlined the seriousness that the British soldiers attached to their mission. Unlike the timidity of the UN force, it was the willingness of the British to bring extreme force to bear that convinced the RUF of the seriousness of the situation and the need to adhere faithfully to the stalled Lome Agreement. The arrest and detention of Foday Sankoh broke the back of the RUF resistance and set the stage for the disarmament, demobilization and reintegration of the rebel fighters by the UNAMSIL. The collection and decommissioning of thousands of weapons therefore proceeded in earnest, . as the RUF became more amenable to the peace process. The elusive peace has substantially returned to the country after a decade of bloody civil war, at the time of writing and general elections that overwhelmingly endorsed President Tejan Kabbah had also been held in the country. And with that, the country now faces the task of reconstruction and reconciliation. Fortunately, the international community seems to have a lot of confidence in the president and has been forthcoming with assistance to cushion the painful transition period.

Notes and References

1. Ibrahim Abdullah, "Bush Path to Destruction: The Origin and Character of the Revolutionary United Front (RUF/SL)," *Africa Development,* vol. XXII, nos. ¼, 1997, 45.

2. Guy Arnold, *Historical Dictionary of Civil wars in Africa,* Lanham, MD and London: The Scarecrow Press Inc., 1999, pp. 237 - 238. See also A. J. Venter, "Sierra Leone's Mercenary War: Battle for the Diamond Fields," *International Defence Review,* vol. 28: no. 11, 1995, pp. 65 - 68.

3. Christopher Clapham, "Sierra Leone: Recent History," **Africa South of the Sahara**, 29th Edition, London: Europa Publications Ltd., 2000, p. 956.

4. Both men were also awarded British knighthood apparently in recognition of their cooperation.

5. Yusuf Bangura, "Understanding the Political and Cultural Dynamics of the Sierra Leone War: A Critique of Paul Richards's Fighting for the Rain Forest," *Africa Development,* vol. XXII, nos. 3&4, 1997, 135 - 136.

6. Abdullah, "Bush Path to Destruction...", 46.

7. Ibrahim Abdullah and Patrick Muana, "The Revolutionary United Front of Sierra Leone: A Revolt of the Lumpenprolitariat," in Christopher Clapham (ed), **African Guerrillas**, 181.

8. This fact was confirmed by the then ECOWAS Executive Secretary Abass Bundu. See *West Africa,* 23 - 29 July 1990, 2165.

9. On the decision to establish and deploy ECOMOG into Liberia, see "ECOWAS Final Communiqué of the First Session of the Community Standing Mediation Committee held at Banjul, ECW/HSG/SMC/1/5/Rev. 1 of 6 - 7 August 1990," see also the covering approval for the operation given by the heads of state in "ECOWAS Authority of Heads of State and Government, Decision A/DEC/. 1/11/90 Relating to the Approval of the Decisions of the Community Standing

Mediation Committee taken during its First Session from 6 - 7 August 1990, Bamako, Republic of Mali, 28 November 1990.

10. Amadu Sesay, "Paradise Lost and Regained? The Travails of Democracy in Sierra Leone," in Dele Olowu, Adebayo Williams and Kayode Soremekun (eds), **Governance and Democratization in West Africa**, Dakar: CODESRIA, 1999, 313.

11. Ibrahim Abdullah, "Bush Paths to Destruction: The Origin and Character of the Revolutionary United Front (RUF/SL)," *Africa Development,* vol. XXII, nos. 3&4, 1997, 68.

12. Paul Richards, **Fighting for the Rain Forest: War, Youth and Resources in Sierra Leone**, Oxford: James Currey, 1996, introduction, xv.

13. Abdullah and Muana, op. cit.182.

14. Abdullah and Muana, op.cit, 182. See also Arthur Abraham, "War and Transition to Peace in Sierra Leone: A Study in State Conspiracy in Perpetuating Armed Conflict," *Africa Development,* vol. XXII, nos. 3 & 4, 1997, 101 - 116.

15. For greater details on this aspect see Jimmy D. Kandeh, "Ransoming the State: Elite Origins of Subaltern Terror in Sierra Leone," *Review of African Political Economy,* No. 81, 1999, especially the section on 'Sobelisation' of the army, 362 - 364.

16. Abraham had detailed this very well from an insider's perspective. See his "War and Transition to Peace...." op. cit. See also Chris Allen, "Warfare, Endemic Violence and State Collapse in Africa," *Review of African Political Economy,* no. 81, 1999, 371 - 372.

17. See transcripts of General Babangida's nationally televised interview on the network of the Nigerian Television Authority in *West Africa,* 22 - 28 February 1993, 282.

18. See Yusuf Bangura, "Reflections on the Abidjan Peace Accord," *Africa Development,* vol. XXII, nos. 3&4, 1997, 234 - 235.

19. See *Africa Research Bulletin,* vol. 36, no. 5, June 23, 1997, 12695.

20. See the full content of the Accord attached as Appendix I in Yusuf

Bangura, "Reflections on the Abidjan Peace Accord" *Africa Development,* vol. XXII, nos. 3&4, 1997, 243 - 252.

21. See the contents of the agreement reproduced in *Accord: An International Review of Peace Initiatives,* (Conciliation Resources, London 2000), pp. 67 - 77.

22. "Peace Agreement Between the Government of Sierra Leone and the Revolutionary United Front of Sierra Leone (RUF/SL)," *Africa Development,* vol. XXII, nos. 3 & 4, 1997, 243 - 252.

23. See Article V of the "Peace Agreement Between the Government of Sierra Leone and the Revolutionary United Front of Sierra Leone," done in Lome on the 7th of July 1999.

24. See Article V of the "Peace Agreement Between the Government of Sierra Leone and the Revolutionary United Front of Sierra Leone," done in Lome on the 7th of July 1999.

25. For critical analysis of the promises and failure of the Lome Agreement, see W. Alade Fawole, *Military Power and Third-Party Conflict Mediation in West Africa: The Liberia and Sierra Leone Case Studies,* Ile-Ife: Obafemi Awolowo University Press, 2001, especially, 27 - 36.

26. An incisive analysis of the failure of the peace process is done by W. Alade Fawole, "Nigeria and the Failure of Peace Making in Sierra Leone," *Africa Insight,* vol. 31, no. 3, 2001, 11 - 18.

27. Jimmy D. Kandeh, "Ransoming the State: Elite Origins of Subaltern Terror in Sierra Leone," *Review of African Political Economy,* no. 81, 1999, 349.

28. See "Report on the Crisis in Sierra Leone," (Memo by Indian Major General Vijay Jetley from May 2000), http://www.sierra-leone.org/jetley0500.html

Section Four: Child Soldiers and Civil Wars in West Africa

Chapter Five: The Phenomenon of Child Soldiers in Armed Conflicts in Liberia and Sierra Leone

Amadu Sesay and Wale Ismail

5.1 Introduction

This chapter investigates the roles and effects of using children in civil wars in West Africa focusing on Liberia and Sierra Leone. It is noted that although the formation of an international coalition against the use of children as combatants especially in the Liberian and Sierra Leonean civil wars has raised international awareness on the practice of child soldiering, nonetheless, too often, the tragic lessons are either overlooked or inadequately addressed. This is in part due to the seductive images of, and emotion-laden responses to child soldiering that often blur the reality. Kofi Annan, United Nation Secretary General, belatedly admitted that much when he declared that "if there is any lesson we can draw from the experience of the past decade, it is that the use of child soldiers is far more than a humanitarian concern, that its impact lasts far beyond the time of actual fighting; and the scope of the problem vastly exceeds the numbers of children directly involved".[1] There is need, then, to examine the underlying socio-economic, political and technological factors associated with the wartime roles of child soldiers with a view to gaining valuable insights into possible post conflict reconstruction programmes in general, the needs of former child combatants in particular, and the likely future security implications of the presence of thousands of former child combatants in civil society.

One of the important messages that the chapter tries to put across, therefore, is that failure to effectively rehabilitate child soldiers in one state will threaten not only the post-war stability and security of such a state, but also that of its neighbours, and indeed the entire sub-region. Accordingly, an imaginative programme of rehabilitation for child soldiers requires a sub-regional approach to complement efforts at the national level. In that regard, this chapter departs from the mainly descriptive extant literature on the subject matter by also incorporating a predictive perspective. It attempts to situate the child soldier phenomenon and the associated consequences within a sub-regional context, with emphasis on West Africa, which is a marked departure from the country-by-country analysis prevalent in orthodox literature. The argument presented here is that the exposure of children to violence constitutes serious threats not only to the targeted opposition groups during the war, but more importantly, to the self-interested recruiters -the State and non-state actors- as the case may be, and the larger society in the post war era. It is contended that the threat often assumes a sub-regional dimension given ill-demarcated and poorly policed borders, the pervasive illegal arms trade and the privatization of security in many countries in the sub-region. Hence children, child soldiers, are also increasingly no longer perceived as future leaders, but as present and future agents of political and economic instability.

As defined here, child soldiering refers to the inclusion or use of any person below the age of eighteen in any kind of regular or irregular force in any capacity including, but not limited to cooks, porters, messengers and anyone accompanying such groups, other than family members.[2] It also includes the use of girls as comfort troops who provide gender based (sexual) services to armed groups, and the use of any child in any war-support capacity such as spying, saboteurs, guards and minefield explorers, and so forth. This definition is consistent with the 1989 United Nations Convention on the Rights of the Child, CRC. Article 1 of that Convention defines a child as "every human being below the age of eighteen years". Furthermore, the African Charter on the Rights and Welfare of the Child, ACRWC, prohibits the recruitment or direct participation in hostilities of anyone under the age of 18 (Article 22).

In understanding the role of child combatants in the civil conflicts in West Africa, it is important to examine the wider (global and African) context of the problem in order to identify the possible international and regional patterns of child soldiering in the post Cold War era. That way, child soldiering in West Africa becomes part of a "whole." In addition to that, the incidence of child soldiering in Liberia and Sierra Leone is examined in succession to set the stage for identifying the lessons that can be learned from their experiences, as well as the future challenges facing individual states on the one hand, and the sub-region as a whole on the other. The concluding section of the chapter provides policy options that could alleviate the threats posed by child soldiers in the post war period in Liberia and Sierra Leone especially, and the entire sub-region in general.

5.2 Child Soldiering in Regional and Global Perspectives

In 1993, perturbed by the horrifying images of six and seven year-olds bearing arms in Uganda, Sri Lanka, Colombia and Liberia, the international community, through the United Nations, instituted an expert study of the phenomenon. The resultant Gracá Machel Report of 1996 set the tone for further international action, especially by Non-Governmental Organizations (NGOs). The advocacy activities by child's rights NGOs in particular, did not only draw attention to the horrifying crimes against children but also to the adoption and subsequent coming into force of the Convention on the Rights of the Child, CRC, in 1989, as well as the 2000 Optional Protocol. Although the Optional Protocol which came into force in February 2002 falls short of a blanket ban on the use of under underage recruitment, it nonetheless narrowed the legal loophole created by Article 38 of the CRC by raising the minimum recruitment age from 15 to 18 years. Article 4 of the Optional Protocol also prohibits the recruitment or use of child soldiers by non-state parties under any circumstances. Finally, the Rome Statute of the International Criminal Court (ICC), (Article 8), declares the enlistment or conscription of children under the age of 15 as a war crime, while the International Labour Organization (ILO) Convention (1982), (Article 2), classifies child soldiering among the worst forms of child labour. Both documents reinforced existing legal provisions protecting the rights of the child.

Despite the plethora of international and regional legal provisions prohibiting the use of under-18 in any direct military capacities, the phenomenon remains widespread. There are over 300,000 children (boys and girls) fighting alongside government armed forces and opposition groups in over 30 countries worldwide. In over 85 countries, hundreds of thousands of more children are also recruited into government forces, paramilitaries and civil militias.[3]

The widespread practice of recruiting children as soldiers cuts across the developed and developing countries, though different patterns exist. The recruitment of child soldiers in developed countries such as the United States (where under 18-year-olds are exposed to military training through programmes such as the Peace Corps and Young Marines, and are eventually recruited into the armed forces), and in the United Kingdom where it is increasingly taking the form of volunteers into military service in a bid to overcome persistent shortfalls in recruitment quotas. In contrast, in most Third World countries where child soldiering exists, recruitment takes the form of conscription and press-ganging. Secondly, even where it is voluntary, the recruitment is closely linked to the often-poor security situation in most Third World countries. In many instances, the pervasive feeling of insecurity usually invites hard choices between victims and victimizers. Moreover, countries in the Third World with the highest child soldier populations are usually also war-torn societies: Afghanistan, Angola, Colombia, Democratic Republic of Congo, El Salvador, Ethiopia, Liberia, Sierra Leone, Somalia, Sri Lanka, and the Philippines, (were) are all victims of protracted civil conflicts.

These countries are also invariably poverty stricken, with a large percentage of their population living below the $2 mark per day. According to the 2002 UN Human Development Report, Colombia, Philippines and Sri Lanka, though classified as having medium human development, still had 36.0, 36.8 and 45.4 percent of their population living below the $2 per

140

day mark respectively.[4] Worse still, Ethiopia and Sierra Leone have an appalling 76.4 and 74.5 percent of their respective populations below the $2 poverty benchmark.[5] In such circumstances, children who volunteer for military service see it as a rare opportunity to benefit from the war economy and recapture a sense of modernity. Oliver Furley in his study of selected African cases studies notes that rather than any convincing political or military ideology; many children joined the factions because of personal gains including prospects for looting.[6] In fact, false promises of $5 and a pair of *Levi's* blue jeans by rebel commanders easily lured poor semiliterate children from rural subsistence-level farming families into childhood soldiering.[7] Another significant consequence of the cycle of war in many developing countries, a child's "social ecologies" described as how a community or family values a conflict, either as a form of social justice, religious duty or ethnic service, for example, could also permit child soldiering. The *Mujahedeen* in Afghanistan, the *Iranian volunteers* in the 1980s, Palestinian children and the *Intifada,* are poignant examples of this phenomenon.

The vicious cycle of conflicts equally creates a round of killings and reprisals that inevitably leads to vengeance, thus providing a rational justification for some children to join military groups. The presence of children in the ranks of the National Resistance Army (NRA) in Uganda, the RUF in Sierra Leone, the NPFL and other factions in Liberia, and the factions in El-Salvador, illustrate the fact that children see their membership of rebel groups as a rare opportunity to avenge the death of family members and loved ones, seek alternative sources of emotional security, and oust corrupt governments/regimes from power. The story of 10 year-old Martin typifies this; "I became a soldier to avenge the death of my father...I came home one day to find him dead..."[8]

Additionally, the technological revolution in weapons' systems, especially the development of light, easily operable and cheaply availably small arms since 1945, has encouraged under-aged soldiering. An estimated 347 to 500 million small arms have been manufactured since 1945, half of which were made between 1980 and 1998. The annual worth of legal trade in (military style) small arms is between $4 and $6 billion, while the black market (illicit) trade is thought to be worth $1 billion a year.[9] The 2001 United Nations General Assembly Session on small arms noted that over 500,000 are killed yearly (1,300 daily deaths) from (military style) small arms.[10] The Russian made AK-47, a family of the Kalashnikovs, for instance, with over 55 million sold since it entered the Russian arsenal in 1947,[11] is held as the most popular small arm. The essential features of small arms- portability (weighs 4.5 kilograms) [12] with only nine moving parts thus requiring minimum infrastructure for maintenance, and their low cost (between $6 and $15 in the informal market across the SSA region, for example)[13] make them readily affordable to factions and for use by children. Afghanistan, El Salvador, Sri Lanka, Somalia, Sudan and Uganda amongst others, are countries experiencing widespread proliferation of small arms and light weapons.

Finally, the wide spread use of child soldiers in the Third World countries is contagious. The contagion effects are the extraneous influences that facilitate the recruitment and use of child soldiers. These effects can be seen at two levels- precedence and geography. Precedent contagion relates to the role played by children in other theatres of war as a factor influencing the forced or voluntary recruitment of children. The geographical contagion refers to the cross-border recruitment and deployment of child soldiers. Most of the wars in the Third World are internal wars involving the mobilization of all available war resources including children, by insurgent and government forces. Most often, these wars often spill into neighbouring countries, allowing for the recruitment of child soldiers across national borders in countries and places such as Afghanistan, Palestinian settlements and the Middle East, DRC, Burundi, Rwanda and the Horn of Africa.

In Sub Saharan Africa, which became synonymous with civil conflicts in the post-Cold War era between 1990 and 2001, there were 57 different major armed conflicts.[14]. Kofi Annan in his 1998 report to the UN Security Council noted that in 1996 alone, 14 of the 53 countries in Africa were affected by armed conflicts, accounting for more than half of all war-related deaths worldwide, and resulting in more than eight million refugees and internally displaced persons.[15] In the 1990s, Sub-Saharan Africa was also host to several "failed states" including Somalia, Liberia, Sierra Leone, Rwanda, DRC and Burundi. Beyond this grim revelation lies the use of children as a war resource in active combat or support capacities.

This is in spite of the fact that Africa has a separate, but complementary child's rights agenda as contained in the 1991 African Charter on the Rights and Welfare of the Child (Article 21) that 'unequivocally' make eighteen years the minimum age for soldiering. Again, although African states have adopted several other legal instruments including the 1996 Yaounde, the 1999 Maputo and the 2000 Accra declarations all of which aim at eradicating child soldiering in Africa, the region continues to play host to the highest number of child soldiers in the post Cold War dispensation. It is interesting to note in that regard, that 24 and 6 states in SSA have signed and ratified, respectively, the Optional Protocol.

Sub-Saharan Africa accounts for over 120,000 child soldiers, representing 40 percent of global estimates, are spread across at least 13 states, including but not limited to Angola, Eritrea, Ethiopia, Liberia, Sierra Leone, Somalia, Sudan and Uganda. The pervasive phenomenon of child soldiers in these countries reaffirms the strong connection between child soldiering, poverty and insecurity (war). Sub-Saharan Africa is the world's seabed of poverty as noted by the 2002 UN Human Development report, which ranks Africa's GDP ($1,690 trillion) and with a negative growth rate (-0.3) lowest in the world.[16] Moreover, about 50 percent of SSA 680 million population lives on less than $1 per day and 34 of its 53 states are among the least developed states in the world.[17]

143

Virtually all the countries in Sub-Saharan Africa have at one time or other been, or continue to be embroiled in civil conflicts. Angola until the breakthrough in the peace process occasioned by the February 2002 killing of Jonas Savimbi (late leader of the opposition UNITA movement) was engulfed in a civil war from independence in 1975. Uganda, another example, has been plagued by armed insurrection from the Lord's Resistance Army (LRA) since 1987. The LRA has abducted over 10,000 children since 1987.[18] The 1998-2001 Ethiopian-Eritrean war was also characterized by large-scale use of children through conscription and press-ganging by the armed forces of Ethiopia and Eritrea. Sudan has equally witnessed a long period of civil war owing to separatist agitation by the Southern Sudanese People's Liberation Army (SPLA) in the last 19 years.

Nonetheless, the most notorious use of child soldiers all through the 1990s and perhaps still, exists in West Africa. The civil wars in Liberia and Sierra Leone brought the menace of child soldiering in SSA into the realm of international public opinion. That children were victims as well as perpetrators of unimaginable crimes such as the amputation of limbs, beheading, gouging of eye balls and the severance of ears and buttocks, shocked the conscience of many people world wide and prompted Kaplan (1994) to describe the war in Sierra Leone as representing the Hobbessian state of nature with irreconcilable cultural and environmental failures.

5.3 Liberia: The Un-ending Story of Child Soldiering

Liberia is undergoing another round of civil conflict barely five years after completing a peace process that led to presidential and general elections in July 1997. Since May 2000, Charles Taylor's regime has been struggling to contain a new insurgency mounted by the Liberians United for Reconciliation and Democracy (LURD) movement. The August 2002 International Crisis Group (ICG) report on Liberia noted widespread use of child soldiers by the government of Liberia and the LURD movement. While David Chea, Liberia's Minister for Defence justified the government's use of children in the now familiar tone of patriotic nationalism, he

144

blamed the United Nations for the failure to reintegrate former combatants, a development he argued, that has led to their easy re-recruitment by the LURD movement[19] although the Movement denied the allegation in a widely circulated press release issued in July 2002. The Movement, instead, drew the attention of the United Nations and child's right groups to the use of hundreds of children, mainly of school age, as defence shields in the western Bomi Hills region by the Monrovia regime.[20] Yet understanding the current wave of child soldiering in Liberia requires a proper grasp of the recruitment, use and consequences of child soldiering in the country's first civil war of 1989-1997.

In December 1989, following nine years of economic down turn, gross violation of fundamental human rights and shadow state practices under President Samuel Doe, the agitation for change in Liberia became violent when Charles Taylor's National Patriotic Front of Liberia (NPFL) led an attack on a border post from Cote d'Ivoire sparking a rebellion that lasted almost eight years. Several other factions emerged in the course of the war, including the remnants of the Armed Forces of Liberia, AFL, the Independent National Patriotic Front of Liberia (INPFL), United Liberation Movement (ULIMO-subsequently divided into ULIMO-K and ULIMO-J) and the Liberia Peace Council, LPC.[21]

Between 1989 and 1997, most of the factors that influenced child soldiering as well as the patterns of recruitment in Liberia followed trends observed across the SSA region. The pre-1989 economic mismanagement by the Doe regime created the debilitating socio-economic conditions-high unemployment; hyperinflation; and acute poverty- that were aggravated by the war and ultimately drove many children into voluntary enlistment. Paul Richards (1995) in his analysis of the Liberian rebellion, identifies youth alienation and economic frustrations of the rural population wherein young teenagers remained largely unemployed, partly educated as a result of the high drop-out rates and limited economic opportunities due to state corruption, as reasons for their involvement in the civil war.[22]

145

The cycle of violence, marked by killings and counter killings, created a chain of vengeance on the part of the children. The initial set of children who volunteered to join the NPFL in the Lofa and Nimba counties, were driven by the reckless counter-insurgency operations of the AFL in early 1990.[23] Moreover, light and easily operable weapons especially the AK47 and Kalashinkovs and the proliferation of these weapons by factions, especially the NPFL's policy of distributing weapons in all areas under its control facilitated the recruitment of children into combat roles.

Contagion effects also influenced the use of child soldiers in Liberia. It is significant to note here that the NPFL and other factions in Liberia had as precedence, the use of child soldiers in Ethiopia, Mozambique, Sudan and Uganda in the 1980s[24]. Apart from that a majority of fighters including children, was recruited from political and ethnic allies (ethnic Mandingoes for instance) across the Mano River area; Guinea and Sierra Leone, as well as Burkina Faso. Although some children joined the factions voluntarily, a majority was forced using 'tabay', described as a form of torture in which a person's elbows are tied behind the back, and the rope is pulled tighter until the ribcage separates. Many others were exposed to 'halaka' or being made to lie flat on their backs with arms and legs suspended in the air while staring at the sun, threatened with death or forced to consent to join the factions in order to stop the killing of innocent family members. Upon recruitment, they were continuously exposed to drugs including amphetamines, cocaine and local alcohol, 'chackla', and were taught to take weapons apart and re-assemble them. Finally, they were exposed to violent films for several hours a day.[25] Between 1990 and 1997, most child soldiers were directly deployed to the frontline as combatants, baits, defense shields and mine detonators. The NPFL's Small Boy Units (SBU) was exclusively for child soldiers, who, with wigs and frogs to enhance their ferocity, were especially noted for their fearlessness and brutality during the civil war.

While most boy child combatants were recruited at the age of 12, and spent between four and five years with the warring factions, girl child soldiers, were recruited mainly as 'wives,' a role that often exposed them to rape and forced labor, [26] although a few did serve as combatants as well. In Liberia, a staggering 30 percent of the 60,000 combatants were children. Most of the 20,000 child soldiers experienced psychological trauma with 28 percent having witnessed the torturing of family members, 63 percent had their homes destroyed and 37 percent sexually abused. Another 51 percent shot an average of 10 people; 11 percent were involved in rape, 17 percent participated in torture sessions, while 3.2 percent practiced cannibalism. [27]

These grim statistics imposed considerable challenges on the Liberian government and child's rights groups during the peace process and in the post conflict period. Unfortunately, however, neither the final 1996/7 Disarmament, Demobilization and Re-integration Programme (DDRP) nor post war peace building efforts adequately addressed the consequences of child soldiering in the country. First, the special physical, psychological and social needs of child soldiers were never recognized under the peace process. The 1993 Cotonou and final Abuja Accords were silent on the rehabilitation of child soldiers. The DDRP was severely under-funded by the international community in the $6.9 million annual budget approved in December 1996, some three months after the commencement of the programme. Even so, the budget was highly inadequate as it represented the cost of just five days of UN peacekeeping operations in the former Yugoslavia. [28]

Under the 1996/7 DDRP, a child soldier, like adult combatants, was to be disarmed, demobilized and reintegrated in 24 hours. A child soldier was also expected to be identified, registered and interviewed within one hour of laying down his arms, and given a thorough medical examination and counseling in another two hours. Apart from the absence of any form of encampment to sever links between child soldiers and wartime command-ers, there were also no transport facilities or escorts available to take children to their final destinations. In the end, only 4,306 child soldiers were demobilized, 89 percent of whom simply wandered away from the demobilization sites to either reunite with former commanders or re-enter the society with their fighting mentality unchanged.

Since 1997, child's right groups like the Save the Children Fund, United Nations Children's Fund (UNICEF), Don Bosco Homes (DBH), Chil-dren Assistance Program (CAP) and United States Agency for Interna-tional Development (USAID) amongst others, have undertaken a holistic planning of their rehabilitation programmes for former child soldiers. The War Affected Youth Support, WAYS, project run by CAP, UNICEF and USAID provide formal training in several disciplines, such as agriculture, shoemaking, soap production and tailoring. The Liberian Opportunities Industrialization Center, funded by the Lutheran World Service, places social workers within communities having un-rehabilitated child soldiers to develop community-based coping (rehabilitation) mechanisms. The Liberian Network for Peace and Development, a consortium of 20 Liberian non-governmental organization (NGOs) funded by the US-based Carter Center, works on the rehabilitation of ex-fighters, including child soldiers. The five DBH centers in Liberia also provide psychosocial rehabilitation together with vocational skills training in carpentry, upholstery, and plumbing among others. The Sarah Daughters' home and My Sister's place programme provide trauma counseling, HIV/AIDS advice and business support for former girl child soldiers.[29]

The achievements of these organizations have been limited by inadequate financing, a development that is linked to the pariah status of Liberia under president Charles Taylor. The complicity of the regime in the gun-for-diamonds trade with the rebel Revolutionary United Front (RUF) in neigh-boring Sierra Leone earned Liberia UN sanctions, including a travel ban on the Liberian political and military leadership and an arms embargo in May 2001. This development, coupled with gross violation of human rights, absence of a true national reconciliation and a return to shadow state practices, under Charles Taylor's regime, has denied the Liberian people of the necessary international goodwill, which is indispensable in any effective post-war reconstruction efforts and programmes. The 1998 Liberian Aid Conference could only secure half of the target $438 million, of which just a little over $20 million has been released. In 2000, the European Union (EU) suspended its post-war assistance package worth $53 million. Moreover, the country is excluded from the Highly Indebted Poor Countries (HIPC) initiative despite its debilitating external debt that stands at $1,064 per capita.[30]

Although the argument that the failure of the guarantors of the peace process in Liberia (UN, OAU and ECOWAS), to ensure the reorganization and restructuring of the AFL and other security agencies, led to the development of private militias and actions that have destabilized the Mano River area is undoubtedly relevant,[31] nonetheless, the biggest challenge to post-war rehabilitation of child soldiers in Liberia has been the policy and attitude of the Taylor regime itself to child soldiers. The NPFL faction demobilized the fewest number (18 percent) of child soldiers under the 1996/7 DDRP, while a majority of the SBU were either integrated into president's Taylor's numerous security units or simply redeployed to Sierra Leone to aid the RUF rebellion in that country. That notwithstanding, the progress in peacekeeping efforts in Sierra Leone by the United Nations Mission in Sierra Leone (UNAMSIL) and other peace building activities including the transformation of the RUF into a political party under the terms (Article III) of the Lome Accord in 2002, have virtually ended the cross border deployment of child soldiers in Sierra Leone by president Charles Taylor. All the same, many children continue to be recruited by the Liberian leader as part of his strategy to contain, if not to crush the LURD rebellion.

149

The August 2002 International Crisis Group, ICG, Report noted the balkanization of president Taylor's security units, including the absence any functional or clear-cut chain of command. A majority of the security agencies, including the Anti-Terrorist Units (ATU), Special Operations Division (SOD), Special Security Services (SSS), the Liberian Marines, Wild Geese and Jungle Warriors, are composed of un-rehabilitated or newly recruited child soldiers, and they all operate as the President's private militia groups.[32] Because of international isolation, reduced or zero foreign investment and insecurity, Liberia's sources of revenue have been narrowed down to rent collection from the Firestone Rubber Plantation and the logging operations of companies, a development that explains the Liberian government's inability to pay the salaries of public workers including the security forces, for months. In the circumstance, government has adopted what can be loosely called a *"pay yourself"* policy, which encourages security personnel to loot and engage in illegal seizures in lieu of unpaid wages, and in order to finance the current war effort. Arising from the self-reward policy and a *"carte blanche"* directive on combating presumed threats to security; members of the security units carry out indiscriminate arrests, rape, and looting as well as widespread destruction of the few existing civilian facilities in the country. The behaviour of the largely un-rehabilitated child soldiers (mostly from ULIMO-K and ULIMO-J), who form the bulk of the LURD movement, is not different from that of government forces either, as they also engage in large scale and indiscriminate looting and destruction of civilian related infrastructures in northern Liberia.

5.4 Sierra Leone: Not Yet *Uhuru*

With the 2002 transformation of the RUF into a political party and a relatively successful Disarmament, Demobilization and Reintegration programme in line with the Lome Accord, there is high optimism in diplomatic and media circles that the civil war in Sierra Leone has finally come to an end. Yet, the challenges of post-war peace building especially how to effectively address the infamous legacies of the civil war abound in the country. Child soldiering is perhaps, a foremost challenge to the Sierra Leonean nation as well as other stakeholders. In understanding the challenges posed by child soldiers to post-war peace and stability in Sierra Leone, it is important to review the phenomenon in some detail.

Sierra Leone has had a chequered post-independence political history. Siaka Steven's long and autocratic rule (1965-1985) was characterized by state theft, graft and political manipulation of unprecedented proportions, developments that instituted patrimonialism in the country. These shadow state practices rebounded on the provision of social services, depriving the youthful population of badly needed social infrastructure, while rendering a vast majority unemployed and desperately poor.[33] Thus, the origins of Sierra Leone's civil war lie in unparalleled economic and political mismanagement. (See also Chapter Three in this volume). The conscious pillaging of state resources by elites, youth alienation coupled with what can be called sub-regional dynamics in West Africa, help to explain the RUF rebellion more than any "irreversible socio-cultural failures".[34] The March 1991 RUF invasion of Kailahun and Pujehun districts in North-Eastern Sierra Leone can be seen, in part, as an attempt to exploit the pre-existing youth discontentment. The estimated number of the child soldiers involved in the civil war in Sierra Leone conflict is put at 10, 000.[35] Child combatants in the RUF/Armed Forces Ruling Council (AFRC) coalition,[36] the Sierra Leonean Army (SLA), and pro-government Civil Defence Forces (CDF) make up this figure.[37] The recruitment of child soldiers by all sides in the war was both by force and voluntary. The internal factors- pre-war socio-economic and political conditions, and the pervading wartime air of insecurity, displacement and sheer survival instincts- explain the rationale behind child soldiering during the war in the country.

Youths joined either pro-government or rebel factions because they perceived soldiering as an opportunity to earn a living in the absence of educational opportunities and the existing limited economic prospects in the country. Abdullah and Muna have argued convincingly, that the RUF was neither a separatist insurgency rooted in any specific demand, nor a reformist insurgency with a radical alternative agenda to the regime it sought to overthrow.[38] Besides, the movement's avowed goal of eradicating wide spread state corruption is contradicted by its own plunder of the country's diamond reserves in the *Kono* fields.

Child soldiers including girls, played active roles during the war with many serving as frontline troops on both sides of the civil war divide. In addition to their gender based sexual roles, girl child soldiers also undertook reconnaissance missions, target assessment and served as liaisons between commanders of battle groups and battlefronts. Isatu, who was abducted by the AFRC at the age of 17, testified that she did not want to go with renegade soldiers but was forced to do so in the end, as they killed a lot of women who refused to follow them into the bush. Isatu ended up being a sexual partner of a combatant and mother of their three-month-old baby. Trained on the use of bayonet, gun, knife, Isatu fought in Faredugu and Makeni, and she admitted cutting off the hands of children and adults, and setting fire to houses with civilians locked inside.[39]

The experiences of child soldiers in Sierra Leone were similar across the various groups and factions. The decadence and indiscipline of the RUF/ AFRC ensured that child soldiers took part in indiscriminate looting, killings, burning of houses, rape, amputation of limbs, fingers, buttocks, gouging out of eyes and severance of ears particularly in 1998 under "Operation No Living Thing" and "Operation Pay Yourself." Not only were children perpetrators, they were also victims- killed either for asking questions or for being reluctant to cut off limbs. The use of cocaine, amphetamine (bubbles), and marijuana was a common occurrence as Sayo recalled: " when I go to the battlefields, I smoke enough. That's why I become unafraid of everything. When you refuse to take drugs, it's called technical sabotage and you are killed".[40]

152

Ibrahim's account further reveals evidence of the traumatizing experiences of child soldiers under the RUF/AFRC: "We were ordered to kill any civilian that we came across. Any fighter or child suspected of being reluctant was severely beaten. We were asked to advance and do everything possible to terrorize the civilians. It was during this period that people's hands and limbs were cut off in Kono, Masingbi, Matotoka..."[41]

The experiences of child soldiers under the Sierra Leone Army, SLA, were also largely traumatic. A majority of them had been recruited by the National Provisional Ruling Council (NPRC) regime in 1992 and were mostly ill trained, undisciplined and saw soldiering mainly in economic terms, the gains that can be made through looting and other nefarious activities during the war. Thus, many of them easily took part in looting, rape and harassment of civilians, as well as illicit diamond mining. Consequently, the civilians labeled them 'sobels' or soldier-rebels, meaning soldiers in the day, rebels at night. Child soldiers under the CDFs had a different experience because of the groups' "No Prisoner Policy," and many child soldiers witnessed the execution of captured rebels. *Brima*, a 12 year-old boy recalled seeing three captured rebels killed; their heads cut off and the children had to take their heads to SLA headquarters as evidence of kamajor effectiveness.[42]

By the time of the November 2000 cease-fire between the government and RUF, a huge number of child soldiers were already suffering from physical injuries, psychological trauma and social alienation. Many, especially those with the RUF, had burns, shrapnel wounds and hernia. The majority of those forcibly seized by the RUF/AFRC rebels had also invariably witnessed the killing of their families and had personally terrorized local communities, including their own. Some of the child soldiers had also taken to cannibalism. Thus in its assessment of the impact of the war on child soldiers in Freetown, *Medicins sans Frontiers noted* that "...[d]eliberately or not, witnessing at least once events such as torture, execution (attempted) amputations, people being burnt in their houses and public rape ... results in traumatic stress or even post-traumatic stress disorder".[43]

The war accelerated the breakdown of social institutions and cultural practices such as the de-mystification of the *Poro* society.[44] For girl child soldiers, the continuous round of unprotected sex made them vulnerable to post-war prostitution,[45] destroyed traditional taboos and incest that regulated sexual relations in indigenous African societies and turned them into vehicles for spreading Sexually Transmitted Diseases (STDs) especially HIV/AIDS.[46] The precarious state of the youths (including children) is captured succinctly in a UNICEF study that concluded that nine years of war had made Sierra-Leone the second most dangerous country in which to be a child.[47]

In spite of the trenchant criticisms of the Lome Peace Agreement which many commentators see as appeasement for several reasons including a blanket amnesty, and access to key government positions including the vice presidency and the ministry of mines,[48] the accord is nonetheless significant for it was the first Peace treaty that expressly catered for the rehabilitation of young combatants as distinct from adult combatants. Article XXX, for instance, called for the recognition of the special needs of child combatants, which must be addressed in the DDR process. The provision is complemented by the rather holistic approach of the broad DDR process itself. For instance, it made provisions for a truth and reconciliation commission, to consolidate peace, human rights and for the establishment of a special fund for war victims, etc. The National Commission for Disarmament, Demobilization and Reintegration (NCDDR), and the National Commission for Reconstruction, Resettlement and Rehabilitation (NCRRR) were also created to co-ordinate the entire DDR process, thus enhancing the rehabilitation of the youth including former child soldiers.

Based on the call for international support and the UN's involvement in the post conflict reconstruction efforts under Articles XXXIII and XXXV, the UNSC in resolution 1270 of October 1999, created the UNAMSIL to monitor and implement the DDR process. In addition, child rights groups also drew up a 15-point Agenda for the rehabilitation of child soldiers. The net result of all this was that first, a National Commission for Children was established to ensure that the rights and welfare of children, youth and women were made a central priority of post war policy making and resource allocation. Second, they called for strict adherence to the child protection component of UNAMSIL's mandate, recognition of, and appropriate actions to be taken in respect of young girls suffering from sexual exploitation and its attendant social stigma, and to intensify campaigns for the release of child soldiers and to stop further recruitment of children for the war effort. Other results include the call to government and communities to reinforce the traditional societal norms that had broken down as a result of the horrific atrocities that were committed during the war, and which had seriously undermined traditional value systems in the country. There also was to be a neighbourhood initiative that would curtail cross-border recruitment and use of child soldiers especially in the Mano River Union zone.

Finally, at the interim care centres and DDR camps, youth combatants were provided with medical care, food and clothing, psychosocial rehabilitation, education and recreation facilities. These services were designed to speed up the re-entry of former child combatants into civil society by enhancing their recovery from physical and emotional injuries, malnutrition, STDs and narcotic drug addiction.

For the child soldiers with the RUF/AFRC or SLA, the initial rehabilitation programme lasted about five weeks; while a shorter period was approved for those with the CDFs, because they had not been separated from their families and communities. The establishment of foster care homes provides avenues for placing orphans with temporary families and/or local communities after they have been disarmed, demobilized and de-traumatized. That way, the tensions and frustration often associated with long periods in rehabilitation homes will be reduced thereby facilitating long-term re-insertion and faster re-integration into civil society. To address the special needs of the girl child soldiers which were highlighted consistently even before 1999, the Forum for African Women Educationalists (FAWE), Sierra Leone chapter, started providing free medical services to sexually abused girls in Freetown, and also opened a care centre for teenage mothers where they would be taught skills such as tailoring and soap making. Between March 1999 and February 2000, FAWE treated over 2000 girl child soldiers, and housed an average of 100 teenage mothers and their children in Freetown[49]

The relief agencies also helped to ease the reintegration into their local communities as they embarked on numerous community awareness campaigns in the country. The March 2000 awareness rally which was organized by CARITAS in Makeni and Freetown was aimed at highlighting the negative implications of child soldiering which it stressed must remain an important component of the DDR and youth re-orientation. Although the resultant Declaration of Commitment to the release of young combatants and child abductees by all the factions was not signed by the RUF, the campaign nonetheless succeeded in sensitizing the larger society about the evils associated with child soldiering.

The involvement of the international community directed attention to the empowerment of the larger family unit economically, psychologically and socially. The World Bank, the World Food Programme, WFP, the European Union, EU, the International Committee of the Red Cross, ICRC, the African Development Bank, ADB and child-focused NGOs, have all been active in local projects in this important area. The WFP and ICRC school feeding and food-for-work programme, for example, provide families with over 30,000 seeds and tools that are important in alleviating the burdens associated with the return of former child combatants into civil society[50]. These programmes offered child soldiers not only psychosocial therapy, but also access to formal education and vocational skills training. The child soldiers' component of the larger DDR programme equally benefited from the increased funding in the late 1990s. Although according to the UN Secretary-general only forty-two per cent of the requested $25 million was realized under the 1999 UN Consolidated Inter-Agency Appeal fund for Sierra Leone, the 2000-appeal fund realized about sixty per cent of the needed $70.9 million by June of that year.[51] In addition, the World Bank, WB, and United Nations Development Programme, UNDP, have equally worked hard to secure bigger donor funding for the DDR process in Sierra Leone. The 1998 WB $100 million DDR assistance and the March 2000 Multi-donor Trust Fund which raised an additional $158 million for the DDR program[52] are very significant examples in that regard.

The United States supports the DDR process both financially and diplomatically with a pledge to underwrite 25 per cent of the total UNAMSIL budget-$782 million- as well as a special $20 million DDR assistance grant. In July 1999, the Canadian government through the Canadian International Development Agency (CIDA) established a $500,000 child protection program to help reunite former child combatants, and to foster forgiveness and reconciliation in communities traumatized by wartime atrocities.[53]

In spite of the moderate successes recorded so far, the rehabilitation of child soldiers faces severe funding problems. While increases have been reported in funding levels by donor agencies and donor governments, overall, the funds remain highly inadequate to meet the myriad needs of former child soldiers in the country. For instance, only $965,000 of the $34m DDR budget for 1998 was allocated to the child soldier component of the national reconstruction programmes. Again, the UN's consolidated humanitarian appeal for Kosovo in July 1999 realized $355 million compared to the paltry $7 million raised for Sierra Leone by the world body.[54] The World Food Program (WFP) also noted a $54 million shortfall in its 2001 budget for Sierra Leone.[55] In short, then, the DDR programme currently faces a $13.4 million shortfall in funding and failure to inject new funds into it in 2002, could seriously affect the rehabilitation and reintegration of former combatants including children, into the civil society, in the country.[56]

This is important because while the CDFs have disarmed, a considerable number of RUF members including children, are yet to demobilize and are still concentrated around their former strongholds in Makeni and Magburaka because of fear of reprisals in their communities of origin. In fact, many RUF fighters including children are still in the streets with very little money and have little prospects in communities that are hostile towards them because of their wartime atrocities. As such, there is a reported rise in the crime rate in some parts of the country. In addition to the above scenario, the Kamajors in the South remain well organized, unwilling to disband, and still retain children in their midst.[57]

Another setback has been the reluctance of major international donors especially the World Bank and IMF, to fund police reform programmes because the police service is associated with the military and they do not want to be seen funding national security agencies. Yet, the present low force level of police manpower, some 7,000, and the absence of basic equipment such as patrol vehicles and communication gadgets, are inconsistent with the maintenance of sustainable peace and security in post war Sierra Leone. The ability of the security forces including the army, to cope with threats to the fragile peace in the foreseeable future, especially a spillover of the civil war in neighbouring Liberia, is seriously questionable given the fact that only 32 of the 150 border crossing points are currently manned.[58] Already, there is a steady influx of armed LURD and pro-government forces from Liberia into Sierra Leone especially, in eastern districts of *Kailahun* and *Kono*, and the southern border near Zimmi town.[59] In fact, in February and March 2002, AFL forces entered Batwono and Bobu, while LURD rebels invaded *Baladu* village, harassed and forced civilians to buy their looted goods.[64]

Above all, there is no guarantee that there will be funding for the rehabilitation efforts beyond the immediate post-war period. That again is a big problem since the rehabilitation of child soldiers is a long-term project. The relative success of UN peacekeeping in Sierra Leone, especially after its setbacks in Somalia and Rwanda, has turned it into a media and public relations showcase that every interested party is quick to be associated with, and claim credit and glory for restoring peace in the war torn country. Yet the challenges of successfully rehabilitating child soldiers and maintaining sustainable peace in Sierra Leone require more than the current media hype and short term commitment, for long term assistance and engagement is needed to prevent a relapse into the conditions that drove children into soldiering in the first place.

In July 2002, the Brussels based ICG Report on the May 2002 elections in Sierra Leone lent credence to the view that it is too soon to declare a victory in that country. The Report noted, in particular, that questions of fairness and coercion continue to trail the elections. Second, that old corrupt practices and "winner-takes-all" politics remain deeply rooted in the country's fragile body politic. Third, that the pattern of voting reveals a dangerous imbalance between the incumbent president and party on the one hand, and the armed forces on the other, because a majority of soldiers voted for the opposition parties. Fourth, that voting patterns were along rival ethnic lines between the opposition Temne in the North and victorious Mende in Southern and Eastern Sierra Leone. This development, the report noted, poses considerable challenges to national consensus building efforts and national cohesion in the post-war period. For a breakdown in national consensus, given the country's political antecedents, could yet generate tensions along ethno-political lines, and could provide a veritable platform for another round of armed opposition during which child soldiers would be used as "firewood."

More importantly, perhaps, are issues of accountability, transparency, and good governance that created the socio-political and economic vacuum, which was exploited by the rebellion, also remain long-term critical challenges to post war stability and even prosperity in Sierra Leone. However, avoiding a relapse into the pre war dysfunctional Sierra Leonean state is a daunting task, in the light of Sierra Leone's grim statistics: 39 years life expectancy rate, 68 percent poverty level, a debt profile equaling 128 percent of GDP and the unenviable position of being the world's poorest country.[61]

5.5 Conclusion

In Liberia and Sierra Leone, pitiable pre-war socio-economic conditions, gross violations of human rights and blatant political mismanagement, provided opportunities that were exploited by the RUF insurgents. The pervasive use of child soldiers is equally tied to the existing overall social, economic and political factors. Yet, there was a contagious dimension to the child soldiering phenomenon in Liberia and Sierra Leone, with precedence playing an important part in both civil wars. There was also what we can call the geographical dimension, since the RUF was directly connected to NPFL controlled territory in Liberia through the numerous smuggling tracts in the forests. Besides, young people in the affected areas often belong to families divided by the border, and usually routinely maintained both Sierra Leonean and Liberian identities before the wars.[62]

In rehabilitating child soldiers, some of the more obvious lapses in Liberia have been corrected by child's right groups in Sierra Leone. Yet, the rehabilitation process is never a "one-off" process. Its failure in Liberia has shown, and emphasized the need for effective planning and success in the short term to achieve initial stability, and long-term engagement for sustainable peace and security. Moreover, the Liberian experience depicts the threats, which un-rehabilitated child soldiers pose to national security and stability in fragile post war societies. Today, thousands of under-aged children are still fighting in Liberia seven years after the formal end of the first round of civil war in that country. Like the first war, there is no doubt that child soldiers can be found on both sides: government forces and the LURD rebel movement.

Ironically, very little interest has been shown by the neighbouring states and the sub-regional body, ECOWAS, in ensuring the successful rehabilitation of child soldiers in the Mano River zone. Expectedly, solely independent child's rights NGOs, friendly foreign governments, and other international donor agencies have undertaken the task of rehabilitating child soldiers. Although ECOWAS produced a manual on child's rights protection for its peacekeeping contingent, it barely addressed the imperative for greater involvement in the larger rehabilitation process itself.

Liberia, Sierra Leone and perhaps Guinea, demonstrate the spill over effects of not only war, but also child soldiering. A majority of the states in the sub-region already show levels of socio-economic and political decay similar to those that contributed to the outbreak of civil war and child soldiering in Liberia and Sierra Leone. Added to that is the huge illegal market in small arms that continues to flourish across the entire SSA region. In June 2002 for instance, the Nigerian Customs Service intercepted 102,000 pieces of live ammunition at the Seme border crossing near Lagos.[63] The illegal arms trade has often aided the increased privatization of security and the emergence of private militia forces in the SSA region.

The ethnic clashes and violence in Cote d'Ivoire and Northern Ghana in 2001 and 2002 respectively, involved large numbers of children. Similarly, the restive oil producing Niger Delta areas of Nigeria continue to witness kidnappings, hostage taking and war-like violence perpetrated by militia forces, which include children. In August 2002 for example, a traditional ruler in Delta State raised alarm over the proliferation of private armies (composed mainly of children of school age) with huge armouries and private detention facilities in the area.[64] All this point to the presence of a precedent contagion in the West African sub-region, yet policy makers see the development first as a largely "Nigerian" rather than a West African phenomenon. Second, it is regarded as violence although in reality it is not much different from some of the events in Liberia and Sierra Leone.

Notes and References

1. See excerpts of Kofi Annan's speech on the eve of the UN General Assembly Special Session on Children (UNGASS) in Child Soldiers Newsletter, Issue 4/June 2002, p. 1.
2. This is similar to the definition adopted at the 1997 Cape Town Symposium on child soldiers.
3. 2001 Global report on Child Soldiers, p.1. Available online at www.child-soldiers.org/report2001/ acknowledgements.html. Accessed 2 August 2002.
4. UNDP, *Human Development Report 2002* . (New York, Oxford University Press; 2002), p. 157.
5. Ibid, p. 159.
6. Furley, Oliver. 'Child Soldiers in Africa' in Furley, Oliver (ed), **Conflict in Africa**. (Tauris, London: 1995) : p. 1.
7. Kelly, D., **The Disarmament, Demobilization and Reintegration of Child Soldiers in Liberia, 1994-1997:the Process and Lessons Learned.** (UNICEF, New York: 1998) p.13
8. See UNICEF, "Children as Victims.", October 2000, search title at www.unicef.org, Accessed 10 November 2000.
9. **Small Arms Survey** (Great Britain, Oxford University Press: 2001), pp. 12-14.
10. See Report of the 2001 UN Summit on Small Arms available online at www.un.org
11. Louise, C., **The Social Impacts of Light Weapons Availability and Proliferation** (UNRISD DP 59, 1995), p. 10.

12. Klare, M., 'An Overview of the Global Trade in Dhanapala et al (eds.) **Small Arms and Light Weapons**. (England, UNIDIR: 1999), pp. 4-5.
13. Small Arms Survey 2001 op cit, p. 17.
14. SIPRI. **SIPRI Year Book 2002: Armaments, Disarmament and International Security**. (Oxford University Press, Oxford: 2002), pp. 63-65.
15. Kofi Annan 1998 report to the UNSC on the causes of conflict and the promotion of durable peace and sustainable development in Africa, para 4. Search title at www.un.org. Accessed 4 July 2002.
16. 2002 UNDP Human Development Report, p. 193.
17. "Africa Presents its Big Idea". BBC News/Africa, 22 July 2001. Search title at www.bbc.co.uk
18. Child Soldiers newsletter, Issue 4/June 2002, p. 4.
19. Liberia's Defence Minister quoted in Kate Davenport, "Liberia's forced recruits", BBC News- Africa, 12 March 2002. Search for title at www.bbc.co.uk/. Accessed 20 August 2002.
20. For excerpts of the LURD press release, see "Taylor accused of using children as human shields," Vanguard, Nigeria 15 July 2002. Available online at www.vanguardngr.com. Accessed 16 July 2002.
21. Aboagye, F., **ECOMOG:A Sub-Regional Experience in Conflict Resolution, Management and Peacekeeping in Liberia**. (SEDCO, Accra: 1999), pp. 50-51.
22. Richards, Paul. 'Rebellion in Liberia and Sierra Leone: A Crisis of Youth?' in Furley, Oliver (ed.) **Conflict in Africa**. (Tauris, London: 1995), pp. 134-141.
23. Human Rights Watch. **Easy Prey Child Soldiers in Liberia**. (Human Rights Watch, New York: 1994), p. 3.
24. Ismail O.M., **The Role of Child Soldiers in National Security: A Comparative Analysis of Liberia and Sierra Leone**, *(unpublished* MPhil thesis, Centre for International Studies, University of Cambridge, 2001)

25. Ismail, O.M., "Liberia's child combatants; paying the price of neglect," *Journal of Conflict, Security and Development*, 2;2 2002: 126-127).

26. Ibid., p. 127

27. Kelly, D., *The Disarmament, Demobilization and Reintegration of Child Soldiers in Liberia, 1994-1997:the Process and Lessons Learned*, (UNICEF, New York: 1998)

28. Ibid., p. 30

29. Ismail, 2002, Op. Cit., 129-130

30. Ibid., p. 128

31. For excerpts of the LURD press release, see "Taylor accused of using children as human shields," Vanguard, Nigeria 15 July 2002. Available online at www.vanguardngr.com. Accessed 16 July 2002.

32. International Crisis Group, **Liberia; Unravelling**. Freetown/Brussels, 19 August 2002, p. 4.

33. Fyle, C. M.(ed), **The State and the Provision of Social Services in Sierra Leone since Independence** (Dakar, CODESRIA: 1993).

34. Kaplan, R. "The Coming Anarchy: How Scarcity, Crime, Overpopulation and Disease are Rapidly Destroying the Social Fabric of our Planet." *Atlantic Monthly*, February 1994, 44-76.

35. Amnesty International., *Sierra Leone: Childhood- A Casualty of Conflict* AFR 51/69/00 (August 2000), 1.

36. The RUF collaborated with the new Koroma military junta following AFRC coup in March 1997.

37. These are hunter-fighter sects, concentrated in the southeastern parts of Sierra Leone and supported the Tejan Kabbah government. Kamajors emerged as the strongest CDF

38. Abdullah, I and Muana, P. 'The Revolutionary United Front of Sierra Leone: A Revolt of the Lumpenproletariat' in Clapham, Christopher ed. **African Guerrillas** (James Currey Limited, United Kingdom: 1998), p. 91.

39. Amnesty International, 31 August 2000, op cit, :p. 9.
40. Ibid. 7
41. Ibid. 4
42. Ibid.10
43. Medicines Sans Frontiers (Holland), *Assessing Trauma in Sierra Leone.* (11 January 2000).
44. For example the pre-war sacred forest used for initiation into the Poro cult became homes to many child soldiers.
45. Nine out of every ten abducted girls were sexually abused. For a general discussion on the treatment of girl child soldiers, see Amnesty International., 'Sierra Leone: War Crimes against Children Continue.' *Press Release.* (19 June 2000).
46. Amnesty International, "Sierra Leone: War Crimes Against Children Continue'" *Press Release.* (19 June 2000).
47. Otunnu, Olara, 'Action to Assist War-Affected Children in Sierra Leone Proposed by Special Representative for Children and Armed Conflict', *UN Press Release* (HR/4432, 14th September, 1999), p. 3.
48. This is the general position of most human rights groups. See Amnesty International., 'Sierra Leone: A Peace Agreement but No Justice.' *Press Release.*AFR51/07/99 (9 July 1999).
49. Amnesty International., 'Sierra Leone: War Crimes Against Children Continue.' *Press Release.* (19 June, 2000.), p. 8.
50. See www.sierra-leone.org, March 2000.
51. United Nations, *Third Report of the Secretary General on the United Nations Mission in Sierra Leone.* UNSC S/2000/1867 (7 March, 2000), para. 57. Available at www.sierra-leone.org/
52. See www.sierra-leone.org, 27 March 2000.
53. "Sierra Leone Building Peace" Search title at www.war-affected.children.gc.ca. Accessed 3 May 2001.
54. Ismail O.M., **The Role of Child Soldiers in National Security: A Comparative Analysis of Liberia and Sierra Leone,** (unpublished

M.Phil thesis, Centre for International Studies, University of Cambridge, 2001), p. 63-65.

55. See www.sierra-leone.gov.sl, March 2000.

56. ICG, *Sierra Leone after elections; politics as usual?* Africa report no 49, Freetown/Brussels, 12 July 2002, 13.

57. See ICG report on Sierra Leone 2002 elections, op cit, 11-13.

58. Ibid., p. 10-12

59. See text of "IRIN interview with Ambassador Oluyemi Adeniji", the UNSC representative in Sierra Leone, 9 July 2002,. Search title at www.allafrica.com. Accessed 10 July 2002.

60. "The jury is still out", Human Rights Watch briefing paper on Sierra Leone, 11 July 2002. Search title at www.hrw.org. Accessed 12 July 2002.

61. According to the 2002 UNDP human development report, Sierra Leone is the poorest country in the world. See also IBRD/World Bank, *World Bank 2002 World Development Indicators* (World Bank, Washington, 2002), 70-125.

62. Richards, 1995: 159

63. See "Customs intercepts 102, 000 pieces of live ammunition," ThisDay News, 26 June 2002. Search title at www.thisdayonline.com. Accessed 26 June 2002.

64. *ThisDay News*, City Diary,(Lagos), Nigeria, 28 August 2002. Also online at www.thisdayonline.com.

Chapter Six: Conflict and Postwar Trauma Among Child Soldiers in Liberia and Sierra Leone

Osman Gbla

6.1 Introduction

A good number of authors have provided disparate theoretical and conceptual perspectives on the issue of child soldiers in African conflicts[1]. Some of these authors tend to link the phenomenon of child soldiers in Africa to traditional cultural initiation and rites of adulthood[2]. This particular view is inaccurate for the simple fact that the use of children in African conflicts contradicts the African traditional perception of children as innocent persons that should not be involved in fighting owing mainly to their age and immaturity[3]. In Africa generally, children are supposed to enjoy love, care and the protection of the family and the community. The art of war is exclusively for the adults. The 1989 United Nations Convention on the Rights of the Child reinforces this view. Article 38(3) of the Convention forbids the recruitment of children under the age of 15 as combatants in conflicts as well as their victimization. Also, the African Charter on Human and Peoples Rights and that on the Rights of the African Child state that no child under the age of 18 should be drafted to take part in armed conflicts.

More recently, it has been asserted that the phenomenon of child soldiers in African conflicts is deeply rooted in the crisis of governance that characterizes most of the post- colonial African states[4]. This crisis of governance has over the years manifested in various forms including, ethnic conflicts over power sharing; incapacity of the state to provide for and protect its citizens; the solitary exercise of political power; mismanagement of state resources, abuse of power and in the collapse of economic and social structures and institutions. The numerous African conflicts into which children are drawn as combatants are a direct symptom of such crisis. In Liberia and Sierra Leone, this crisis was intensified by the ascendancy to power in 1980 by Samuel K. Doe and the adoption of one party rule in 1978 under the leadership of Siaka P. Stevens respectively. These oppressive and repressive regimes in Liberia and the single- party dictatorship in Sierra Leone resulted in their angry violent dismantling by rebel forces that recruited children.

We are also convinced that the effective rehabilitation and reintegration of these children into civil society in both countries would only be meaningfully realized by the convenient blend of Western and African traditional approaches. The exclusive use of Western methods has proved unsuccessful in Mozambique, an African country. The main reason for this failure is that the strategies failed to take into consideration the socio-cultural, religious and political realities of the African societies and settings. [5]

Western definitions and understanding of distress and trauma, of diagnosis and healing and of childhood differ greatly from those of African societies with different ontology, social and cultural patterns. Furthermore, the Western-oriented approaches concentrate more on the perpetrators rather than the victims. They fail for instance, to sufficiently prepare the communities to accept back their prodigal sons and daughters. Against this background, there is the need to build the capacity of the family members and the communities to which the former child soldiers would return. For example, in many African societies including Liberia and Sierra Leone, people believe in ancestral spirits and their crucial role in both the causation and healing of mental health problems. In this context, it would be productive to make use of the services of traditional healers and local artisans in the rehabilitation and reintegration of former child soldiers in these countries.

6.2 Background to the Civil Wars in Liberia and Sierra Leone

Liberia and Sierra Leone are two of the three West African countries (including the Republic of Guinea) that make up the Upper Guinea region also known as the Mano River Union Tri-state Area. The region is bounded in the Northeast by the Futa Jallon highlands. It is well watered by many rivers including the Mano River after which the name Mano River is coined. The approximate total population of the three states is fourteen million (14,000,000).[6]

There are over twenty ethnic groups in the region among which are the Mandingoes, Fullas, Mendes, the Kissis, Limbas, Temnes, Vais, and Golas. Significantly, some of these groups- the Mendes, Vais and Golas- remained divided by the current international boundary between Liberia, Sierra Leone and Guinea. This situation partly explains the closer and cordial relationships between and among some of these groups at certain times especially across their common borders. In spite of this fact, these groups belong to different linguistic groups- the Mandes and the West Atlantic. This fact also suggests that all the ethnic groups do not belong to the same original stock although there have always been long and closer interactions between and among themselves.[7] The three states also constitute the Mano River Union (MRU), an economic integration initiative established in 1973 with the objective of improving the living standards of their people through the harmonization of their development efforts in the economic, social and cultural spheres. Although saddled by many problems, the first decade of its existence witnessed some positive steps designed to develop the sub-region. It successfully implemented, for example, the sub-regional industrial strategy linking the produce marketing boards of the three states and the Mano River Postal Union.

The sub-region was plunged into violent armed conflict in December 1989 following the rebellion of Charles Taylor against the Government of Samuel K. Doe in Monrovia, Liberia. The war, like many others in Africa, was attributed to many causes. One of these is the unresolved cleavage between the settlers - Americo-Liberians and the indigenous tribes - the Khrans, Gios, Manos, etc. C.M. Fyle reiterated this point when he remarked that the Liberian rebellion was a calculated move by Charles Taylor to recover the privileged position the Americo-Liberians once enjoyed.

The Americo-Liberian minority ethnic group controlled and dominated the post-independence politics of Liberia from 1847 to 1980. During their reign, the indigenous groups were excluded and marginalized. This led to disenchantment and disillusionment. Among many other things, the marginalization precipitated the 1980 coup that was masterminded by Master Sergeant Samuel K. Doe, a Khran from Nimba County. The coup brought to an abrupt halt the long, insensitive and exclusive regime of the Americo-Liberians in the country. The regime of Samuel Doe was also closely associated with the ruthless exercise of power and the brutal massacre of political opponents. Thus the Liberian war, like many others in the African continent, cannot be attributed to any one cause. It was triggered by a combination of social, economic, ethnic and external factors.

Sierra Leone too became a theatre of war in March 1991 following the attack at Bomaru by a small band of Revolutionary United Front (RUF) fighters aided by members of Charles Taylor's National Patriotic Front of Liberia (NPFL). The war was initially interpreted as an offshoot of Taylor's war of terror in Liberia by most commentators. Charles Taylor had since the early 1990s become very displeased with Sierra Leone following the country's pivotal role in the Economic Community Monitoring Group's (ECOMOG) operations in Liberia. As the headquarters of ECOMOG was also based in Sierra Leone, it was used as the launching pad by ECOWAS to restore peace and stability in Liberia. Charles Taylor perceived the West African force as a calculated design to frustrate his political ambition of becoming the head of state of Liberia. Accordingly, Sierra Leone became a target of his terror. He had in fact openly threatened that Sierra Leone too would taste the bitterness of war. Unfortunately, the threat was not seriously taken by the All People Congress (APC) reign of Joseph Saidu Momoh - a mistake that has cost the country dearly in both human and material terms. Taylor also had an envious eye on Sierra Leone's diamonds as a very valuable resource to fund his war of terror.

The RUF claimed that they took up arms to liberate the country from the claws of the dictatorial and oppressive regime of the APC. The APC, which ruled the country from 1968 to 1992, first under Siaka Stevens and then, Joseph Momoh, his handpicked successor, was corrupt, inept and insensitive to democratic principles. In his attempt to annihilate any form of opposition to his regime, Stevens employed a series of repression techniques, draconian press laws, killings and arbitrary detention of political opponents. To ensure the success of his divide and rule policy, tribalism and nepotism, State appointments were not based on merit but on connection. Members of the Ekutay Club - a northern-based association predominantly of Limbas from Binkolo during the regime of Momoh occupied key political positions in government. There was also rampant corruption and mismanagement of scarce resources as the leaders and their henchman fed fat on the sweat of the people by embezzling public funds most of which were kept in foreign banks.

In spite of the above startling revelations about the APC regime, Sankoh's war of terror against defenseless citizens cannot be seen as a war of liberation. It can best be described as a criminal insurgency. This is mainly because the rebels have not been able to articulate a coherent set of political objectives. Instead they engaged in indiscriminate killing and harassment of innocent civilians, massive destruction of life and property, as well as the illegal exploitation of natural resources (diamonds, cocoa, coffee, etc).

Other writers and commentators have attributed the war to the government's inability to improve the welfare of the youths who remained predominantly illiterate, unemployed and directionless.[8] Majority of them are vulnerable to the manipulations of selfish politicians. In fact the APC government used youths as thugs to unleash terror on political opponents,

171

and later provided a fertile ground for the recruitment of the RUF's fighting force. Although majority of them were forcefully conscripted and trained to become merciless killers, some youths joined the movement voluntarily as a way of ensuring their security and survival.

The war was engendered by a combination of interrelated economic, social, cultural, political and external factors. To attribute it to any one particular cause will obfuscate any objective analysis of its true nature and manifestations. In summary, both wars have not only continued to claim the lives of many innocent people but have also created a formidable barrier to the rapid socio-economic and political development of the Mano River Union sub-region.

6.3 Child Soldiers in the Civil Wars in Liberia and Sierra Leone: The Unenviable Legacy

The extensive and indiscriminate use of children (both males and females) as combatants in the Liberian and Sierra Leonean conflicts is alarming. Available evidence in Liberia estimated that 6000 children below the age of 15, approximately 10% of all fighters participated in the conflict.[9] In Sierra Leone; available statistics suggest that up to 12% of the estimated 45,000 fighters in the war are children. Out of a total of 50 Sierra Leonean ex-child soldiers randomly selected for interview, 88 percent were boys and 12 percent were girls. As Table 6.1 below reveals, a sizeable proportion of the respondents, 12 percent were below 15 years of age, while the majority, 48 percent, were aged 15-19. It is important to note that six years prior to the survey (by 1995) nearly all the respondents in these two age brackets had not attained age 15, meaning that at least 60 percent of the ex-combatants interviewed were below age 15 when they got involved in the conflict.

Table 6.1: Ex-child Soldiers by Age Group and Sex

Age group	Male		Female		Total	
	Number	Percent	Number	Percent	Number	Percent
10-14	4	9.1	2	33.3	6	12
15-19	20	45.5	4	66.7	24	48
20-24	18	40.9	0	0	18	36
25-29	2	4.5	0	0	2	4
Total	44	100	6	100	50	100

Source: Field Survey, 2001

Depending on the time they got involved, those aged 20-24 at the time of interview 36 percent, were either in the age group 15-19 or part of those aged below age 15.[10]

The armed insurgent groups - the NPFL and United Liberation Movement of Liberia, (ULIMO) in Liberia and the RUF in Sierra Leone - are the ones most noted for the recruitment of children. This strategy was deliberately adopted because children, unlike adults, could be easily recruited, trained and programmed to accept the lives they are conditioned to live[11]. It is therefore not surprising that Charles Taylor's NPFL had a unit popularly known as the "Small Boys Unit". This group of young fighters was the most fearless and atrocious during the war in Liberia.

Government forces and their allies in both countries also had children below the age of 15 in their rank and file. In Sierra Leone, the government and their main backers- the Civil Defense Forces (CDFs) - especially the Kamajors, the Gbethis and the Donsos to a much lesser extent, also recruited children. Majority of the children voluntarily joined to defend their villages and communities against the insurgents especially after realizing that the national army colluded with the rebels to wreck havoc instead of protecting innocent civilians[12].

Considering the general African perception of children as innocent persons that should not take part in warfare, what is responsible for the unprecedented use of children as combatants in both wars. For many analysts, children are preferred because they are easy to manipulate and to programme to undertake any chores.[13] There is also the assumption that they possess excessive energy that can be conveniently utilized to realize the nefarious objectives of the insurgent groups. They can, for example, carry out orders with more vigour and enthusiasm especially after being trained and programmed by the adults[14]. Furthermore, majority of them see involvement in war as something exciting and therefore worth exploring. They think that fighting is a game as well as a source of gaining respect and dignity in society. For some others, joining the war as combatants is the only sure guarantee of their survival and sustenance as they have lost their parents and source of livelihood. In both countries, some of the children voluntarily joinea in order to be assured of their daily survival and that of their families[15], while others were simply abducted.

The survey carried out among child soldiers for this chapter in Sierra Leone, supports the claim that majority of them joined the various factions voluntarily (especially those that are pro-government). As Table 6.2 below shows, 72 percent of all respondents stated that they joined their respective factions voluntarily. However, 50 percent of the respondents claimed they were forcibly recruited into the RUF compared with none for the government forces; and only 14.3 percent of the pro government CDF.

174

Table 6.2: Means of Joining the Fighting Forces by Child Soldiers (%)

Means of Joining	Fighting Force				
	Government	RUF	CDF	AFRC	Total
Voluntary	100	50.0	85.7	0	72.0
Forced	0	50.0	14.3	100	28.0
Total	100 (14)	100 (20)	100 (14)	100 (2)	100 (50)

Source: Field Survey 2001

In particular, forced conscription was the most pronounced tactic of the rebel factions. Majority of the child soldiers were forcibly abducted by the armed insurgent groups from schools, playing fields and during raids on villages and towns. One of the children interviewed by Wessell in Sierra Leone[16] disclosed that he was abducted after the rebels had killed his parents. Fighting factions especially the rebels, forced their way into houses, caused mayhem and threw residents into disarray and took away the children in the midst of the chaos and panic. For most of the children who joined the fighting forces (both government and rebel) voluntarily, however, they believed that it would provide them with both security and survival. The possession of a gun is usually perceived as a big mark of achievement that will give them respect and dignity in the community. Kole Omotosho's account of the Liberian situation supports this view: "...O.J a boy of twelve years old, joined Charles Taylor's Small Boys Unit because he was hungry and felt the need for protection and survival."[17] The sample survey shows that ex-child soldiers were influenced to join one faction or the other for a variety of reasons (apart from being forced), ranging from the urge to defend the community or self to revenge and material benefits to be derived from carrying gun.

Table 6.3: Reasons Given by Child Soldiers for Joining Fighting Forces (%)

Reason	Fighting Force				
	Government	RUF	CDF	AFRC	Total
Economic	0	10.0	0	0	4.0
Revenge	0	20.0	28.6	0	16.0
Forced	0	20.0	0	0	8.0
Community (or Self) defense	100	20.0	71.4	100	60.0
Other	0	30.0	0	0	12.0
Total	100 (14)	100 (20)	100 (14)	100 (2)	100 (50)

Source: Field Survey, 2001

As Table 6.3 above indicates, majority of former child soldiers interviewed, 60 percent, stated that they were induced to join the war by the urge to defend their community or simply for personal defense. For the various factions, 100 percent of the Government ex-recruits, 20 percent of RUF and 71 percent of CDF advanced this as their reason for joining. Some (4%) for the economic benefits they expected from using the gun to loot or extort from others. It is interesting to note that of all those interviewed, only RUF ex-child combatants, 10 per cent, gave economic benefit or gain as a reason for joining any of the factions. What is also important to note about the survey result is the fact that the children believed that with a gun in their hands, there is power to coerce and force others, including adults, to give up their food items, and comply with their orders.

A sizeable proportion of both the RUF and the CDF ex-child soldiers gave the urge to avenge the death of some relative killed by the other faction as their motive for joining, 20 percent and 28 percent respectively. In Sierra Leone, majority of the children who voluntarily joined the Civil Defense Forces, (CDFs) especially the Kamajors and Gbethis, were influenced by the desire to avenge wrongs done to them and their families and also to participate in the defense of their country. For example, Omaru Bangura, age 18, told the authors during the field interviews, that he was compelled to join the Gbethis to revenge the painful death of his uncle in the hands of the RUF. He further disclosed that he would go all out to see that the rebels are completely wiped out in his village.[18] Another interesting finding is that none of the respondents, with the exception of the RUF (20%), stated that they were forced to join the faction they belonged to. This clearly reinforces the widely held belief that the RUF depended heavily on force or coercion as a recruitment strategy.

After recruitment, the next gruesome stage of the ordeal of these children is their initiation into the culture of violence and terror - they are trained to be fearless fighters and remorseless killers. The long periods of parades, beatings and traumatic scenes of killings characterized the trainings in the camps. As their first baptism in the art of killing, some of them were ordered during trainings to kill a colleague who tried to escape. After being drugged and indoctrinated, some were taken back to their villages and asked to kill relatives, rape women and loot property.

In further attempts at inculcating the culture of violence and fearlessness into the minds of the new 'recruits', they were made to watch Rambo and Kungfu videos. A. Sesay underscored this point in his reflections on the phenomenon of child soldiers in Liberia in the following words:

> Child soldiers have been engaged in various forms of initiative violence inculcated from routine exposure to brutality reinforced by repeated showing of Rambo and Kungfu videos, and further facilitated by the regular abuse of drugs.[19]

As Table 6.4 below illustrates, 28 percent of all ex-child soldiers interviewed in Sierra Leone confirmed that they were drugged and exposed to Rambo films as a way of making them fearless. As expected, all the respondents were exclusively RUF ex-child soldiers and represented 70 percent of the faction's child soldiers that were interviewed for the study.

177

Table 6.4: Method of Initiating Child Soldiers by Fighting Forces (%)

Initiation Method	Fighting Force				
	Government	RUF	CDF	AFRC	Total
Drugged/violent films	0	70	0	0	28.0
Forced to shoot/kill	100	30	14.3	100	48.0
Indoctrination	0	0	85.7	0	24.0
Total	100 (14)	100 (20)	100 (14)	100 (2)	100 (50)

Source: Field Survey, 2001

The majority of the children (48%) however stated that they were forced to shoot (or kill) during their initiation. The data show that all government ex-child soldiers went through this method of initiation compared with just 30 percent for former RUF child soldiers, and 14.3 per cent of CDF ex-child soldiers.

During trainings, the children were also introduced to various forms of superstitious practices all of which were designed to reinforce their desires to kill and their invincibility.[20] 12 year old Mohamed from Ropet village in Northern Sierra Leone, and a former fighter with the *Gbethis*, told the authors that the "country cloth" (Ronko in the Temne language[21]) which he usually put on when going to the war front protected him "from the white man's bullets" provided he observed all the rules, regulations and rites associated with it, including abstinence from sexual intercourse with women. During the interview, he revealed that after going through the initiation ceremonies of the Gbethis, they were all asked to put on their Ronkos, lined up in a straight line and were then fired at in turn to test their potency. These revelations are very instructive in explaining some of the most violent atrocities committed by the former child soldiers who were not only trained to be remorseless fighters but were also indoctrinated to believe that they are bullet proof.

In Sierra Leone, indoctrination as a method of initiation - making recruits to believe that going through some ceremonial rites would make them immune to bullets- as presented on Table 6.4 above - is most common in the CDF. Being forced to shoot or to kill was another method of initiation experienced by a sizeable proportion of all the respondents (48%); 100 percent of Government ex-child soldiers, compared with 30 percent of the RUF and 14.3 percent of the CDF.

The civil wars in Liberia and Sierra Leone have no doubt impacted negatively on many children in both countries. Some were not only involved in active combat but were also compelled to kill, while others got killed on the front lines. As shown on Table 6.5 below, most of the ex-child soldiers interviewed (80%) stated that they were involved in the war as active fighters. The situation is virtually the same for each of the factions involved in the war in Sierra Leone: government forces, 71.4 percent, RUF, 80 percent and CDF 85.7 percent. Consistent with their role as active fighters, the overwhelming majority of ex-child soldiers interviewed (88%), as presented on Table 6.6, confessed to having killed someone during the war.

Table 6. 5: Role Played by Child Soldiers in each of the Factions in the Civil War in Sierra Leone (%)

Role	Fighting Force				
	Government	RUF	CDF	AFRC	Total
Active fighting	71.4	80.0	85.7	100	80.0
Porter	0	10.0	14.3	0	8.0
Intelligence	28.6	0		0	0	8.0

Table 6.6: Acts of Killing by Fighting Force (%)

Whether Killed	Fighting Force				
	Government	RUF	CDF	AFRC	Total
Yes	100	80	85.7	100	88.0
No	0	20	14.3	0	12.0
Total (N)	100 (14)	100 (20)	100 (14)	100 (2)	100 (50)

Sources: Field Survey, 2001

100 percent of all Government ex-child interviewed said they had killed some one compared, with 86 percent and 80 percent for their CDF and RUF counterparts, respectively.

A good number of the child soldiers were victims of both physical and sexual abuse at the hands of the older soldiers. In Liberia, for example, most of the child soldiers were tortured which resulted in severe damage to the arms. A good number of the ex-child soldiers who are now in interim care centers awaiting reintegration, have been psychologically scarred by the violence, which they witnessed and endured at an intimate range. Others are physically and mentally incapacitated by the torture and drugs, which were some times forcibly administered to them. The girls among them, who were frequently beaten and raped, are also physically and mentally disturbed.

6.4 Post-war Trauma Stress Disorder and Former Child Soldiers

One of the most pathetic effects of the Liberian and Sierra Leonean wars on the children who actively participated in them as combatants is post-trauma stress disorder. The most visible symptoms of this phenomenon are anxiety, depression, hyperactivity, aggressive behaviour, withdrawal, bed-wetting and recurrent nightmares. Unfortunately, both countries lack the resources and facilities to adequately deal with this problem. Furthermore, most of the strategies employed to address the phenomenon are overwhelmingly western- oriented, sometimes, with very little or no consideration for the current local situations of the ex-combatants, such as culture, religion, traditions etc.

In the survey conducted for the study between July and November 2001, each of the 50 ex-child soldiers was asked to state the ways in which their involvement in the wars had impacted on their minds. As Table 6.7 indicates, the majority (60%), said their minds are troubled (or tormented) whenever they remembered the atrocities they had been involved in. 86 percent of government, 50 percent of RUF and 43 percent of CDF respondents confirmed this experience and phenomenon. Being easily angered recorded the next highest frequency, but was evident in the government and CDF ex-recruits only -14 percent and 29 percent respectively. Next is the tendency to be aggressive; 20 percent and 29 percent for the RUF and CDF - respectively.

Table 6.7: Effects of the War on the Minds of former Child Soldiers by Fighting Force

Effect	Fighting Force				
	Government	RUF	CDF	AFRC	Total
Easily angered	14.3	0	28.6	0	12.0
Troubled mind	85.7	50.0	42.9	100	60.0
Aggressive	0	20.0	28.6	0	16.0
None	0	30.0	0	0	12.0
Total	100 (14)	100 (20)	100 (14)	100 (2)	100 (50)

Source: Field Survey, 2001

It is significant to note that respondents who said that the war had no effects on the minds were exclusively former RUF fighters, 30 per cent.

The type of trauma experienced by the ex-child soldiers however depends on many other important factors. These include, among others: their mode of recruitment and training, type of activities engaged in during the war, their age at the time of recruitment and the Length of time spent in

181

the bush[22]. The ex-child soldiers interviewed were asked to state which memory if any they persistently had in terms of their war time experiences.

Table 6.8: Memories of Acts of Violence Committed by Ex-Child Soldiers

Type of violence	Fighting Force				
	Government	RUF	CDF	AFRC	Total
Killing of civilian	0	30.0	28.6	0	20.0
Killing of enemy	0	0	28.6	0	8.0
Arson and looting	0	10.0	28.6	0	40.0
Physical assault/rape	100	10.0	0	0	4
None	0	50.0	14.3	100	28.0
Total (N)	100 (14	100 (20)	100 (14)	100 (2)	100 (50)

Source: Field Survey, 2001

It is clear from Table 6.8 that arson and/or looting accounted for the highest number of violent acts committed by former child soldiers, 40 percent of all respondents. 29 percent of CDF and 10 percent of RUF of the respondents identified this type of violence. 20 per cent of all respondents acknowledged killing of civilians, although it accounted for 30 percent and 29 percent respectively, between the RUF and CDF ex-child soldiers. Significantly, only 10 per cent of respondents admitted rape and physical assault as a type of violence they committed while in the bush.

Majority of the child soldiers who were actively involved as combatants in the wars were severely traumatized, very troublesome, and very difficult to handle. On the other hand, those who wore uniforms but served in non-combatant capacities such as porters and intelligence gatherers are less traumatized and very easy to handle. Unfortunately, both countries lack the facilities and resources to adequately treat those child soldiers who are adversely affected by their participation in the wars.

Susan, a Sierra Leonean who was recruited by the RUF at the age of 12, attributed her traumatic experience to her forced participation in the death of another child soldier that tried to escape but was later caught. She vividly narrated the ordeal this way:

182

A boy tried to escape, but they caught him. They told us the other new children; we should kill him with sticks. I refused, I knew him from my village. They told me they would shoot me if I refused; they pointed the gun at me so I had to do it. All the time the boy was asking me, why are you doing this. I said I had no choice. After he was dead they made us smear his blood on our arms and told us that we should not fear death and so we would not try to escape. I still dream about the boy from my village. In my dreams he is saying I killed him for nothing and so I am always crying.[23]

Susan's testimony confirms the very traumatic experiences of young persons of her age, for a number of reasons. First, witnessing the scene of the painful death of a close acquaintance is not only scarring but also mentally and psychologically disturbing. Second, Susan's active participation in the inhuman act was also harrowing. Finally, in an African traditional setting like that in Liberia and Sierra Leone, there is the general belief that the spirits of the dead have the capacity to mentally disturb those who caused their deaths.

6.5 Post-war Trauma Healing and Reintegration of Former Child Soldiers

Post- war trauma healing, social rebuilding and reintegration programmes in both Liberia and Sierra Leone put premium on addressing the needs of child-ex-combatants. The Lome Peace Accord signed between the Sierra Leone Government and the RUF on July 7, 1999 specifically recognized the significance of children and their place in the rehabilitation and reintegration programmes. Article XXX of the Agreement stipulates that:

The Government shall accord particular attention to the issue of child soldiers. It shall, accordingly, mobilize resources, both within the country and from the international community, and especially through the Office of the UN special Representative for Children in Armed Conflict, UNICEF and other agencies, to address the special needs of these children in the existing disarmament, demobilization and reintegration processes.[24]

The same article provided the framework and mandate for specific assistance that targets children who participated in the conflict. The care, welfare and protection of child combatants are therefore the responsibility of all stakeholders. It was against this background that the Sierra Leone Government's National Committee for Disarmament, Demobilization and Reintegration (NCDDR), committed itself to the speedy rehabilitation and reintegration of the former child soldiers in the country.

In Liberia, although the various peace agreements did not specifically mention how the needs of former child soldiers could be met, nonetheless, the government, in close collaboration with non-governmental organizations and UN agencies, designed and implemented programmes catering for these children. Organizations like Don Bosco, Abused Women and Girls (AWAG), the Catholic Relief Service (CRS) and Save the Children, are very outstanding in efforts to rehabilitate and reintegrate former child soldiers into civil society in Liberia.

In Sierra Leone, one of the leading community - based local NGOS with an impressive track record in handling the post-trauma stress disorder of child ex-combatants is the Children Associated with the War (CAW). Unlike most other projects for ex-child soldiers' psychological rehabilitation and reintegration, which require a lot of planning time, the CAW programme emerged spontaneously in response to the plight of children associated with the war in Sierra Leone. In this context, the beneficiaries arrived before programme planning, funding and staffing arrangements were made.

One of CAW'S most popular interventions in the management of post-trauma stress disorder in ex-child combatants is a Six-month Psychological Rehabilitation (SPRP) Programme. As a short term recovery measure, the SPSR seeks to provide post-trauma services and treatment for the former child soldiers within a residential type of setting - an interim care center - for a period of six months to stimulate/foster psychological, social, health and educational recovery and healing after demobilization. At the two CAW interim care centres visited by the researchers, they found psychologists, home administrators, home masters, several teachers, and nurses, caregivers, cooks and security personnel. While at the Centres the ex-combatants are exposed to a series of post-trauma stress disorder healing programmes. One of these is psychotherapy - a method of treating mental illness that requires the sufferer to talk about his/her painful memories as a way of healing. In explaining the role of psychotherapy in handling the post trauma stress disorder of child ex- combatants, Philip Kamara, a Child Protection Officer in Sierra Leone, noted that the caregivers in the Centres give a friendly ear to the children's stories of horror. The Centres were also found to be providing guidance and other forms of help to the young people and help them recover some of the pleasures of childhood through games and sports[25]

It must be pointed out, however, that these methods of treating post-trauma disorders in the former child soldiers have their limitations. For instance, the six months spent treating the ex-combatants is very short given the extent of the physical and mental damage done to the child soldiers by the long years of war and violence perpetrated by them or against them. But more importantly, the treatment is overwhelmingly based on western psychological approaches in an African environment that is drastically different from those in Europe or America. In these parts of the world, the definition and understanding of distress and trauma, its diagnosis and healing processes are totally different from those in Africa.[26] It is little wonder, then, that the approach failed in Mozambique, when it was experimented with the first group of child soldiers that came from the RENAMO Camps. It is doubtful, then, if the present post-trauma stress treatment given to ex-child soldiers would succeed in Sierra Leone. The problem, really, is that western psychological healing methods locate the causes of psychological distress within the individual, and therefore devices responses, which are primarily based on individual therapy. Healing and recovery in such a situation is achieved through helping the individual to come to terms with the traumatic experiences, and the treatment is normally done in private.

In Liberia, just as in Sierra Leone, majority of the NGO's dealing with post-trauma stress disorder of the former child soldiers employ Western psychotherapy methods of healing. The Children Assistance Programme (CAP) in Monrovia, Liberia, one of the NGOs involved in the treatment of ex-child soldiers also provides a residential setting where the children are prepared for eventual reintegration into civilian life. Unlike CAW in Sierra Leone, CAP kept the children in the transit centers for a period of three months during which period they are placed under the supervision of trained counselors who offer them advice and encouragement. The former ex-combatants are also provided with games and sport facilities to take care of boredom at the Centre.

Although the modern psychotherapy methods discussed above can be useful in a non-western setting, it should also take into account the local culture and perception of mental disorders and their successful treatment. It is clear, for example, that majority of the people in Liberia and Sierra Leone, like those in many other African countries, believe that war-related psychological trauma is linked to the anger of the sprits of those killed during the war.[27] The socio-cultural settings of both states would therefore seem to emphasize the role of ancestral sprits and other spiritual forces in both the causation and healing of mental heath problems. In southern Mozambique, for instance, these spirits, referred to as 'mipfhukwa', are generally believed to have the power to harm those who killed or mistreated them in life. In Sierra Leone, they are called' mompilas' '(ghosts)', and are also believed to have the power to hurt and torment those involved in their deaths. Consequently, people in both countries, especially those in the rural areas, still believe that the dead have a role to play in the day-to-day affairs of the living. These beliefs and perceptions must be taken into account if the treatment of former child soldiers for post trauma stress disorders in Liberia and Sierra Leone is to be successful.

As observed above, it is important to bear in mind that a significant number of people in both countries are influenced in their behaviour by the belief that those who participated in wars, killed, or saw people being killed, are polluted by the spirits of the dead. This is because such people are believed to have displeased and angered the sprits and that if the aggrieved spirits are not appeased their wrath will befall both the perpetrators and their communities. This point is very important because unlike modern psychology, which locates the state of mental confusion and effects only on the individual perpetrator, the traditional African post-war trauma healers locate the confused mental state and confusion on both the perpetrator and the community as a whole. It is against this background that the people in both countries strove in varying degrees, to appease the spirits of the dead in order to save both the perpetrators and their communities from the wrath of these spirits, usually through a series of ritual cleansing ceremonies.

At Ropet Village in Northern Sierra Leone, Amadu Sesay, a 15-year-old youth who was conscripted by the RUF had to undergo a ritual cleansing ceremony after he returned to his community. The elders in his family, including his grand father Pa Santigie Sesay, a famous traditional leader, took the boy to the bush where a hut had been built using grass for the boy's cleansing ceremony. On entering the hut, Amadu was asked to undress himself that is, to take off the clothes he used to put on while with the RUF. The hut and the clothes were then set alight while an adult relative helped out the boy quickly. The burning of the hut and the clothes and everything else that the boy brought from the war symbolically represents his sudden break from an evil past. Immediately thereafter, a chicken was sacrificed to the sprits of the dead and the blood smeared around the ritual place. It is important to note that the sacrifice was carried out to appease the sprits and to give peace to both the boy and his community as a whole.

This traditional technique of healing post-trauma stress disorder in demobilized child soldiers has very important traditional messages. In the first place, it lends credence to the popular African belief that the dead still have a very crucial role to play in the lives of the living. Second, it buttresses the point that in most African societies, there is room for rehabilitating and accepting back a wicked child in line with the adage that 'there is no bad bush to throw away a bad child'. And finally, it reflects the typical African perception that links the happiness as well as the sorrow of an individual with that of his community as a whole.

It is not surprising therefore that most of the post-trauma healing; rehabilitation and reintegration programmes for child ex-combatant in Liberia and Sierra Leone emphasize sensitizing and empowering the family/community members of the children. This approach is informed by the realization that the success of such programmes will be determined largely by the acceptance of the ex-child soldiers by their families/communities. This explains in part why CAW'S programmes in Sierra Leone also made extensive use of local resources - both human and material, in treating the former combatants. Its Family Tracing, Reunification, and Reintegration programme (FTRR) for example, reflects this thinking. Specifically, the programme seeks to trace and reunite the children with their family members, and stresses the need for them and their communities to accept back their children. Besides that, the programme also promotes peace and reconciliation education, and helps to correct family/community prejudices and misconception about the former child soldiers. Further more, the Organization helps to empower family/community members through micro credit facilities, small income generating activities and the strengthening of local educational and training facilities.[28]

Another very important component of CAW's post-trauma stress disorder healing strategy in Sierra Leone that seriously takes local conditions into account is the educational and skills training programme. The programme is informed by the Organization's belief that training is therapeutic - it helps to build self-confidence, respectability and redirects the child's energy to more useful channels and activities. In addition to that, it is believed that training builds hope and empowers the child to earn a living and meaningfully contribute to the development of society. CAW therefore engages the children in local apprenticeship training schemes in carpentry, tailoring and construction work, etc.

In Liberia, the government works closely with NGO'S and local communities to embark upon public awareness campaigns geared towards sensitizing the communities to accept the demobilized child soldiers once again into civil society. In the urban areas, the services of community leaders are utilized both in the sensitization and healing processes of former child soldiers. However, the communities' reactions towards the ex-child soldiers are mixed. That is, while some residents are sympathetic towards the ex-combatants, others are hostile. Significantly, communities that are sympathetic expressed willingness to accept the child soldiers while the hostile ones refused to do so.

Addressing the post-trauma stress disorder states of former child soldiers, their general rehabilitation and reintegration into civil society in both countries have not been problem-free as already pointed out. One of the important constraints is that majority of the former child soldiers in the two countries are returned to families and communities that had been economically and socially disoriented by long years of devastating and debilitating wars. The infrastructure - schools, hospitals and community buildings (court barries- communal meeting places very popular in rural Sierra Leone- churches and mosques) for example, were either looted or destroyed during the war. Furthermore, majority of the parents of the former child soldiers had been rendered financially bankrupt and socially incapacitated because they lost their sources of income and livelihood, as well as their other possessions in the war. In the face of these difficulties, both parents and communities are not in a position to adequately address the needs of the former child combatants — education, health, clothing, etc— following their reunification and reintegration into their local communities. The rehabilitation programmes in both countries are also hampered by severe lack of trained manpower, especially psychiatrists and trauma healers. In Sierra Leone, for example, there is only one professionally trained psychiatrist to handle the numerous cases of post-trauma stress disorders in the former child soldiers. Owing to the numerous and highly publicized atrocities committed by the former child soldiers against their families and communities, some families and communities are unwilling to accept them back into their fold. Another serious constraint is that some families and communities continue to associate the ex-child soldiers with murderous warring factions in the war, a situation that has also hindered the smooth implementation of the rehabilitation and reintegration programmes in many parts of the country. Finally, lack of infrastructural facilities and financial resources has also seriously hampered efforts directed towards the control, if not elimination, of post-trauma stress disorders in former child soldiers in both Liberia and Sierra Leone.

6.6 Summary and Recommendations

This chapter critically examined the issue of child soldiers in West African conflicts with particular emphasis on the treatment of post-trauma stress disorders in demobilized child soldiers in Liberia and Sierra Leone. It discussed the background to the conflicts in both countries as well as the factors that accounted for the involvement of children as old as seven years in the wars in both countries. The chapter also assessed the various methods employed to handle the post-trauma stress disorders of ex-child soldiers, highlighted and discussed some of the problems hampering their successful rehabilitation and reintegration into civil society in both countries.

A recurring theme in the chapter is the view that an effective, sustainable and proactive post-trauma healing, rehabilitation and reintegration programme for former child soldiers in both countries will be one that is conceptualized and implemented taking into account the local environment, families and communities of the ex-child soldiers. In this regard, the chapter noted that the community's acceptance of the child soldiers is a vital element in their successful reintegration into civil society. We noted that although young girls were also captured and forced to participate in the civil wars in Liberia and Sierra Leone, the reintegration polices and programmes developed in both countries did not adequately address their own peculiar needs. In fact majority of them are/were marginalized by the disarmament, rehabilitation and reintegration programmes at all levels in the two countries. Finally, the chapter highlighted a number of constraints facing efforts to successfully treat post-trauma stress disorders in the former fighters, as well as their general rehabilitation and reintegration into their families, communities and civil society at large. These include the poor economic and social conditions of their families and communities' lack of financial resources and the necessary professional expertise.

In the light of the study findings, the following recommendations are being put forward to ensure effective treatment of post-trauma stress disorders in former child soldiers, and their successful rehabilitation and reintegration in both Liberia and Sierra Leone.

- The two governments as well as members of the international community should undertake to effectively tackle the root causes of the conflicts into which children were drawn as combatants. One way of doing this is to enthrone democracy and good governance in the two countries. That means, among many other things, putting in place open, transparent and inclusive political systems predicated on the rule of law, an impartial justice system and efficient management of meager and scarce state resources.

- Since the unenviable predicaments of Liberian and Sierra Leonean children are deeply rooted within the fabric of the culture and customs of both countries, there is need for culturally appropriate intervention programmes that will make extensive use of traditional healers, secret societies and religious leaders, in the treatment of post trauma stress disorders in former child soldiers.

- In Liberia and Sierra Leone, the family and community are very essential components of civil society. Accordingly, it is important to give them strong support in order to enhance the social acceptance and tolerance of the former child soldiers. This is especially urgent given the fact that most of the affected families and communities are economically and socially dislocated by the civil wars. Effective programmes designed to empower these families and communities must include interest free revolving loan schemes, funding for income-generating projects especially in agriculture, petty trading, rehabilitation and reconstruction of schools, health centres and other community based infrastructure.

- Given the devastating impact of the two civil wars on girls and thousands of disabled children, post-conflict trauma healing, rehabilitation and reintegration programmes should endeavour to incorporate their special needs in terms of their health and medical care, education, counseling and protection from societal rejection. At the moment, these children run the risk of being marginalized and rejected by their communities.

- Both the developed and developing countries should, as a matter of urgency, ratify the Convention on the Rights of the Child and the Optional Protocol on children in armed conflicts. These are two very important legal documents that provide the international legal framework that would stop the recruitment and abduction of children into conflicts, a phenomenon that has become rampant in the post Cold War era in Africa.

Notes and References

1. For more on this phenomenon, See Furley, O. (1995), "Child Soldiers in Africa"; in O. Furley (ed), **Conflicts in Africa,** London/ New York: Tauris Academic Studies.

2. Richards, P. (1996), **Fighting for the Rain Forest: War, Youth and Resources in Sierra Leone,** Oxford: IAT, James Currey and Heinemann.

3. Albert, I. O. Albert, Isaac, O (1999), 'Child Soldiers and the Security Discourse in Africa'. Paper presented at the Biennial Congress of the African Association of Political Science (AAPS), Dakar, Senegal, p3.

4. Richards, P. op. cit

5. Honwana, Alcinda (1999), "Negotiating Post-War Identifies: Child Soldiers in Mozambique and Angola" CODESRIA Bulletin, No 1 and 2

6. **Africa South of the Sahara Regional Surveys of the World,** 1999.

7. Fyle, Magbaily, C. (1999), Indigenous **Political Culture and Democratization in Upper Guinea,** Africa Zamani, New Series No2 pp99

8. Abdullah, I. (1997), "Bush Path to Destruction: The Origin and Character of the Revolutionary United Front (RUF)" *African Development,* Vol. XX 11 Nos. ¾

9. Kaikai, Francis (2000), 'Disarming and Demobilizing Child Soldiers in West Africa- Developing Appropriate Interventions: The Sierra Leone Experience,' A briefing paper pp1

10. ILO (1995), 'The Reintegration of young ex-combatants into Civilian life'. Paper prepared for the Vocational Training Systems Management Branch, ILO, Office Geneva, 1995.

11. Honwana, A. op.cit, 7

12. The Civil Defence Forces (CDFs) refer to all the civil militia groups that sprung up in Sierra Leone in the mid1990s to challenge the insurgents. They are mostly groups of hunters referred to differently in the various districts and regions in the country. In the Southeast, they are known as the Kamajors (hunters) while in the north they are called the Gbethis or Kapras (the Temne name for hunters.)

13. Honwana, A. op. cit. 6
14. Furley, O. (1995), "Child Soldiers in Africa"; in O. Furley (ed), **Conflicts in Africa,** London/ New York: Tauris Academic Studies, and Human Rights Watch/Africa and Human Rights Watch Children's Project, **Easy Prey: Child Soldiers in Liberia.**
15. Albert, I. O. op. cit. 3
16. Wessells, M,(1997), "Child Soldiers", in *Bulletin of the Atomic Scientists,* Chicago, November / December
17. Quoted in Albert, I. O., op. cit. 5.
18. Interview with Omaru Bangura, aged 18, and member of the Gbethis at Ropet Village in Northern Sierra Leone; conducted on the 10th September 2001, at Magbosie.
19. www.c-r.org/cr/accord/sesay
20. See Albert, I.O. op. cit. 6
21. The Temnes are the second largest ethnic group in the country. They are found mainly in the North and in Freetown, the capital.
22. ILO, op. cit.
23. Ibid, 10
24. Lome Peace Accord, 1999, 224.
25. Interview with Mr. Philip Kamara, a Child Protection Officer in Freetown; on 21st November 2001 in Freetown.
26. Honwana, A. op. cit. 9
27. Ibid; 10
28. ILO, op. cit.

Section Five: Post-War Reconstruction in Liberia and Sierra Leone

Chapter Seven: Multilateral Agencies and Post-conflict Peace Building in West Africa: Lessons from Liberia and Sierra Leone

Osman Gbla

7.1 Introduction

Liberia and Sierra Leone were plunged into violent civil wars in 1989 and 1991 respectively. Both wars, like many others in Africa, were triggered by a number of interrelated internal and external, political, economic and social factors. Prominent among these was the failure of governance and the concomitant socio-economic, political, ethnic and generational exclusion experienced in both countries. Sierra Leone's political landscape especially between 1967 and 1991 alternated between a long period of authoritarian civilian and military regimes.[1] During these years, members of the political class and their cohorts did not only attempt to annihilate the opposition but also perfected the art of political patronage, intolerance, corruption, and nepotism, which inevitably led to socio-economic decline in the country.

In much the same way as neighbouring Sierra Leone, Liberia's political system was characterised by long years of oppressive oligarchic and ethnically centred leadership.[2] Beginning in 1847 when the country became politically independent and republican, the political, economic and even religious structures were controlled predominantly by the minority Americo-Liberian group made up of former free (as well as descendants) of American slaves (1847-1980). During their long grip on power in the country, the majority indigenous African peoples and ethnic groups - Khrans, Gios and Manos, Mandigos, etc- were not only cruelly oppressed but were also politically excluded, a development which, among other things, precipitated the civil war of 1989[2].

The long years of bitter civil war in both countries; (Liberia (1989 - 1997) and (Sierra Leone 1991 -2001), were accompanied by massive destruction of both human and material resources. In Sierra Leone, estimates of the total number of people killed range from 20,000, to 75,000[3]. The number of displaced persons was also alarming: over 357,000 while the Sierra Leonean refugee population was estimated at a million.[4] Hundreds of others were maimed, amputated and rendered physically and mentally incapacitated. In Liberia, the death toll from the civil war and the degree of displacements were equally alarming. Available data estimated that about 200,000 Liberians died in the war while between 750,000 and a million were internally displaced and made refugees respectively.[5] It is therefore not surprising that both wars severely traumatised, demoralised and psychologically weakened their populations.

The conflicts also contributed significantly to the dislocation of the economies as well as the physical infrastructure and social facilities of both countries. In Sierra Leone, the civil war pushed the economy to the brink of total collapse by seriously disrupting productive economic, agricultural and commercial activities. The major sources of government revenue, including diamonds, gold and agriculture were adversely affected. Medical, educational, and social infrastructure in both rural and urban Sierra Leone were completely devastated. Hundreds of thousands of houses and community centres were completely destroyed. The experience in Liberia was not better either. Indeed, while destruction of property in Sierra Leone was confined mainly to the rural areas of the country, Freetown, the capital, was left almost intact when compared with the destruction of Monrovia, its Liberian counterpart. Accordingly, majority of the returnees in both countries went back to communities without basic social infrastructure, and which, were also reluctant to forgive, accept and reconcile with the perpetrators of the destruction and violence, the ex-combatants and child soldiers.

The two civil wars, expectedly, adversely affected the legitimacy of the governments and their ability to effectively govern their people. In both countries, basic institutions of government including the executive, the legislature, the judiciary and local governments either ceased to function effectively in some parts of the countries, or were faced with serious crises of legitimacy. In Sierra Leone, for example, central government authority in the rebel-controlled districts of Kailahun, Kono and Bombali was completely replaced with rebel administration for many years. Consequently, post-conflict peace building initiatives in Liberia and Sierra Leone would have to emphasize the re-establishment and strengthening of governmental institutions both at the centre and local levels, their legitimacy and authority.

The spill over effects of the conflicts on neighbouring Guinea in particular and the West African sub-region in general are equally alarming. The influx of Sierra Leonean and Liberian refugees into Guinea had devastating effects on its fragile economy and social infrastructure and political stability. The refugees brought to the fore fundamental issues of insecurity, the fragility and porosity of state borders and the flagrant abuse of human rights, especially of children and women. For some time, the refugees were the target of terror and harassment by Guinean authorities and citizens who blamed them for causing insecurity in their country. The fighting between and among dissident forces and the governments of Guinea and Liberia along their common borders contributed in no small measure, to sub-regional insecurity, mistrust and suspicion. In that regard, post-conflict peace building efforts in both countries must therefore emphasise initiatives that will restore sub-regional stability and trust among West African leaders. This is important because peace in both Liberia and Sierra Leone would be incomplete without peace in the entire sub-region.

Against the above background, multilateral agencies working for the restoration of peace in Liberia and Sierra Leone must galvanise their efforts to also ensure sub-regional peace in West Africa. This is both urgent and important given the fact that some of them, including the United Nations, the OAU and ECOWAS, are also moral guarantors of peace agreements signed by the two countries. A classical case in point is the Lome Peace Agreement signed by the Revolutionary United Front, RUF and the Government of Sierra Leone on July 7 1999. The next section provides a detailed examination of the role of some of these agencies in post conflict building efforts in the two countries.

Multilateral Agencies and Post-Conflict Peace building in Liberia and Sierra Leone

War-torn Liberia and Sierra Leone are currently faced with a number of disparate tasks all of which are related to post-conflict peace building. Some of these tasks are aimed at ensuring the implementation of peace agreements, reviving their ruined economies and fragile governance structures, the repatriation and resettlement of internally displaced persons (IDPS) and refugees. Both countries also have to sufficiently prepare their civil societies and war traumatized populations to forgive, accept and reconcile with the ex-combatants. However, and considering the nature and magnitude of these tasks, as well as the present states of their economies, the two countries, on their own, effectively meet the huge challenges without international support and assistance. Not surprisingly, a plethora of international actors are involved in the various post-conflict peace building efforts in the two countries (see also Chapter Four in this volume).

Prominent among the many multilateral agencies currently involved in post-conflict peace building efforts in both Liberia and Sierra Leone, are the United Nations, the World Bank, the International Monetary Fund, IMF, the African Development Bank, ADB, the European Union, the Islamic Development Bank, the defunct Organisation of African Unity (OAU), and ECOWAS. Friendly Governments like those of Britain, America, Nigeria and Guinea are playing critical roles in post war peace building efforts especially in Sierra Leone. Its is the efforts of mainly these international actors, and community- based organizations that are currently propelling the daunting task of post-conflict peace building programmes in both countries. However, much attention will be focused on the roles of the United Nations, the World Bank, the British government and selected community- based organizations in post conflict peace building initiatives in Liberia and Sierra Leone.

7.2 The UN and UNDP

Like many other multilateral agencies, the UNDP Post-conflict peace - building programmes anywhere in the world, are guided by clearly defined mandates. The Organization's Executive Board's Decisions, General Assembly Resolutions, Global Summits, Country Co-operation Frameworks, and Advisory Notes generally prescribe these mandates among many others. General Assembly Resolution 44/211 for instance, emphasizes national capacity building, the importance of national goals and principles and the need to promote the integration of women in all aspects of the development process as priority interventions.[6] In fact, the Organization's central mandate - Sustainable Human Development - requires that it focus attention on restoring social, economic, and political stability.

The UNDP, in close working co-operation with the World Bank, usually concentrates in post-conflict countries on efforts not only to address the needs of the affected populations but also on the factors that contributed to the outbreak of the conflicts in the first place. In the case of Liberia, the Organisation tried, first, and working closely with ECOWAS, to facilitate not only the signing, but also strict implementation of peace agreements. Some of the most outstanding of these agreements include that of July 25, 1993, and the Akosombo Accord of December 1994. One notable feature of the agreements is that they emphasized a variety of confidence building measures ranging from cease-fires through disarmament and de-mobilization to the holding of general elections.

Against the above background, there was a dire need for the swift intervention of multilateral agencies like the United Nations not only to provide the necessary funds and logistics but also to supervise and monitor the implementation of these agreements. The result, among other things, was the creation of the United Nations Observer Mission in Liberia (UNOMIL) in September 1993. The team, made up of 303 observers and support personnel worked closely with ECOMOG to monitor and verify the implementation of the demilitarization components of the Agreement.[7] By April 1994, UNOMSIL's Observers were stationed at 27 of the 39 projected team sites to monitor activities at border crossings, airports, seaports and other sensitive areas (UN Document S/1994/463). Despite the limited success of ECOMOG/UNOMIL in Liberia, it is obvious that the co-operation and collaboration between the United Nations and ECOWAS especially, was very instrumental in building confidence between and among the warring factions in Liberia. The two organizations, ECOMOG and other agencies, facilitated the July 1997 presidential and parliamentary elections in Liberia. Working together with the World Bank, the United Nations provided funds, election materials and other resources for the conduct of the elections. Together with ECOMOG and ECOWAS, it created the environment in which Liberians were given the opportunity to cast their votes and free from intimidation by overseeing the conduct of the elections.

In addition to facilitating the elections, the UN also played (and is still playing) a crucial role in supporting Liberia's national reconstruction programme. At a special donors meeting held in Paris on 7th April 1998, bilateral and multilateral donors including the UN pledged $230m in support of the country's two-year national reconstruction programme.[8] The UNDP alone pledged $58m to support specific programmes on poverty reduction, capacity building, and good governance. The agency fully supported eight of Liberia's thirteen counties in the areas of basic social services like health, education and shelter. UNDP and WFP provided funds for a two-year training programme to facilitate self-employment among the youth and former combatants.

The United Nations has been directly involved in the peace building process in Sierra Leone, although it did not start as early as was exp.. 'ed. Rather, if left much of the efforts to ECOWAS and merely endorsed the measures adopted by the sub-regional organisation[9]. It was not until 1995 that the UN began to take serious and co-ordinated efforts in support of the peace building efforts in the country. That year saw, for example, the appointment of a special envoy to the country by the Secretary General, Mr. Berhanu Dinka an Ethiopian. Among other things, the envoy was entrusted with the responsibility of working with both the OAU and ECOWAS to negotiate a settlement and to return the country to civilian rule after the 1992 military coup.

The UN again encouraged the military regime to implement its timetable for the return of the country to democratic rule, made possible through financial and material support from the Electoral Unit of the United Nations secretariat and the UNDP. Besides, and working closely with the OAU and ECOWAS, and through its special envoy, the United Nations was instrumental in facilitating first, the disengagement of the NPPRC military regime from power, and the holding of parliamentary and presidential elections in 1996. The United Nations also provided substantial funding for the two National consultative meetings that were held between August 1995 and February 1996. These meetings by and large enabled Sierra Leoneans to express their views on the electoral process and the future of their country. Some of the conclusions reached at those conferences paved way for the 1996 elections that brought President Ahmed Tejan Kabba to power. Finally, the United Nations provided funds, ballot papers as well as observers to monitor the elections.

At another level, the UN, the OAU, ECOWAS, the Commonwealth and the World Bank, played crucial facilitating roles in the signing and the implementation of the various peace agreements signed by the RUF and the Government of Sierra Leone. The United Nations Secretary General's special envoy, Berhanu Dinka, for example, helped to negotiate the signing of the November 1996 peace agreement in Abidjan. The Agreement, which is popularly known as the Abidjan Peace Accord endorsed the need for initiatives that are aimed at the rehabilitation, reconstruction and development of the nation and its people. It made provision for example, for the disarmament, demobilisation and reintegration of ex-combatants and for the setting up of a Commission for the Consolidation of Peace (CCP) in post conflict Sierra Leone. The CCP had representatives from both the government and the RUF, and was entrusted with the responsibility of monitoring and implementing the Abidjan Accord. The United Nations again provided funds, logistic support and facilities for setting up and equipping the CCP office. Unfortunately, the implementation of the agreement was stymied by the intransigence of both the RUF and the military coup of May 25, 1997.

It should also be noted that the UN played a leading role in the signing of the Lome Peace Accord between the Government and the RUF/SL on July 7,1999. That agreement is important because it formed the basis for the formal end of the war in January 2002. It is significant to also note that the Accord made provision for the observance of an immediate ceasefire; the disarmament, demobilisation and reintegration of ex-fighters; the establishment of an inclusive government and the setting up of committees to monitor the implementation of the provisions of the agreement[10]. Furthermore, the UN and the rest of the international community were required to play a crucial role in ensuring the strict implementation of the Accord. It is to its credit that the organization stood firmly behind the Accord and the central government authorities in Freetown ensuring that the fragile peace was maintained while further negotiations between the RUF, the government of Sierra Leone and other stakeholders continued.

At the 4054th meeting in October 1999, the Security Council adopted Resolution 1270 which established the UN Peace keeping Mission in Sierra Leone, UNAMSIL. With a Force of some twenty seven thousand men at its peak, the Mission was the biggest that the world body has ever mounted anywhere in the world. It was, among other things, to practically implement the provisions of the Lome Accord, especially those pertaining to the ceasefire, disarmament, demobilisation and reintegration of former fighters and returnees.[11] UNAMSIL was to initially share the responsibility of implementing the Accord with ECOMOG, but the arrangement did not last as ECOWAS had to withdraw ECOMOG not long after the Force was deployed.[12] Nonetheless, the cordial relationship between the UN mission and ECOWAS in their peace building efforts in the country was rather exemplary and commendable, compared to their experience in Liberia. It is particularly instructive to note here that the UN laid a lot of emphasis on the military initiatives, while ECOWAS was particularly active in ensuring the continuation of the political negotiations that would eventually bring the bloody civil war to a peaceful end.

With a force of about 27 men UNAMSIL played a very crucial role in providing confidence-building measures between the Government and the RUF. In March 2000, for example, Ambassador Oluyemi Adeniji, the new Special Representative of the Secretary General in Sierra Leone, requested ECOWAS to convene a peace meeting in Bamako, the Malian capital. The meeting, which brought together the principal stake holders: UNAMSIL, the Government of Sierra Leone, the RUF and AFRC, paved the way for the open and frank discussions that followed and prepared sufficient ground for confidence building between the government and the RUF. Significantly, all parties agreed to dismantle illegal roadblocks, return the weapons and ammunition seized by the RUF from Guinean troops and the immediate removal by the RUF of all obstacles to the deployment of UNAMSIL. Together with the National Committee for Disarmament, Demobilisation and Reintegration (NCDDR), the UNAMSIL disarmed and demobilised over 45,000 ex-combatants, set up reception centres for the disarmed combatants and destroyed arms and ammunition recovered or surrendered by the ex-fighters, and ensured the security of the areas vacated by the rebels.

All the same, and like previous UN-peace keeping missions in other parts of the World, UNAMSIL had to contend with many problems. First, was its unfamiliarity with the Sierra Leone terrain and which contributed significantly to their humiliating abduction by RUF fighters. Five hundred peacekeepers were shamefully disarmed and captured by the rebels not long after they entered the country. Besides that the limited mandate of the peacekeepers constrained its ability to effectively deal with the rebels. The mission was also beset with logistical, financial and managerial problems, all of which hampered its initial operations in the country.

Another UN post-conflict peace building intervention initiative in both Liberia and Sierra Leone worthy of consideration is the Preventive Development Project. Started in the mid 1990s, the project focused attention on the resettlement and reintegration of Internally Displaced Persons, ex-combatants and returnees. The Project provided emergency relief and assistance including farm tools and implements to the target groups at their various communities in the two countries. The prime objective was to enhance local capacities for strengthening post conflict peace building momentum and sustainable development. In Sierra Leone, specifically, the Project played a very crucial role in the resettlement of returnees in the Kenema, Pujehun and Tonkolili districts. The pilot experiment was however interrupted by the May 25th 1997 military coup by Major Johnny Paul Koroma. Its successor programme, the Peace and Development Initiative, PDI, was also designed to promote national consultations and consolidate the momentum for ensuring peace and stability in the country.

7.3 The World Bank

Working closely with the United Nations and other multilateral agencies, the World Bank has also been very instrumental in promoting Post-conflict peace building initiatives in both Liberia and Sierra Leone. The Bank's Programmes emphasize rebuilding physical infrastructure, aid co-ordination, strengthening policy dialogue and reform; and mobilizing resources from diverse sources in the war torn countries. Most recently, the Bank concentrated its efforts on the demobilization and reintegration of ex-combatants, the resettlement of displaced persons and returnees especially in Sierra Leone. In implementing most of these programmes in the country, the Bank liaises closely with the UN and other agencies already on the ground in both countries.

In Sierra Leone, the World Bank has played and is still playing a crucial role in the practical implementation of the Community Re-integration and Rehabilitation Project (CRRP). This post-conflict peace-building project seeks, among other things, to address the short-term post-conflict needs of ex-combatants, refugees and Internally Displaced Persons (IDPs), and the communities to which they were returning. The major objective of the programmes, it would seem, was to enhance security, social stability and economic revival by helping former combatants, the population and communities affected by the conflict return to normal productive lives. Accordingly, the CRRP is made up of two major components: the Economic Recovery Support Fund (ERSF) and the Training and Employment Programme (TEP). The former helps to facilitate the recovery of local communities through the restoration of basic economic and social services, while the latter supports social and economic reintegration of ex-combatants through counseling, training and employment creating initiatives.

In close collaboration with the African Development Bank, ADB, the World Bank ensured the implementation of the CRRP by providing seed funds totaling approximately US$41.3 million. The CRPP project has over the years been very instrumental in ensuring a modicum of peace, tranquility and sustainable livelihood for returnees in Sierra Leone, by giving them a sense of belonging and hope and by keeping them positively busy as much as possible.

7.4 Britain

As the country's former colonial master, Britain more than any other country, has contributed significantly to Sierra Leone's post-conflict recovery and peace-building efforts. Under the guidance of the British Defence Forces, the British Government played a very important and leading role in retraining and restructuring the Sierra Leonean army. Under very stringent and rigorous screening and recruitment processes, potential recruits were given equal opportunities to compete with one another for enlistment in the Force. Individuals from all the country's geopolitical regions were encouraged to join the 'new look' army in a bid to put in place an efficient, loyal and disciplined army. A significant number of soldiers have successfully passed out since the retraining programme was launched in early 2000. It would be recalled here that the national army of Sierra Leone collapsed following the coup of may 1997, and the country had to start almost from scratch rebuilding its army.

The British Government has also been helping in restructuring the Sierra Leone Police Force. Under the command of a British Inspector General of Police, Mr. Keith Biddle, the Sierra Leone Police Force was being sufficiently equipped to respond effectively and promptly to the safety needs of the population more than ever before. There has also been a significant change in public perception of the police, while its image as a corrupt institution is gradually disappearing. There is now, for instance, a disciplinary and investigation office at Police Head Quarters to handle public complaints about the Force's conduct and to take prompt confidence-building corrective measures. These important changes and developments will no doubt contribute significantly to the enhancement of law and order in the country.

7.5 Community Based Organizations

Community-based organizations, CBOs, have, expectedly, been very instrumental in championing post-conflict peace building programmes in both Liberia and Sierra Leone. Being very close to the people and very much aware of the socio-cultural, economic, historical and political realities of these countries, they are sometimes more appropriate than international agencies in promoting post-conflict peace building efforts. In Sierra Leone, one of the leading community-based organizations with a very impressive track record in the area of peace building is the National Alliance Against Drug Abuse And Poverty (NAADAP). As a registered indigenous organisation established in 1994, it is committed to the task of drug abuse prevention, poverty reduction and peace building in both rural and urban Sierra Leone. One of its most successful efforts in Sierra Leone is its awareness raising programmes through conferences and workshops on the issues of war, drug abuse and poverty. In October 1995, for example, it successfully organized a national conference on the theme:' Youth Education for Poverty Reduction and Peace building in Sierra Leone'. The conference enabled various stakeholders in the peace process in Sierra Leone to share experiences on the way forward for peace in the country. It is also currently running a skills training centre for young men and women in Northern Sierra Leone. In 1998, it also organized a Post-Conflict Trauma Healing and Peace Building workshop for rural returnees in Northern Sierra Leone, in order to sensitize rural returnees on the need for forgiveness and reconciliation. It is important to note that the activities of community based organizations have helped in no small measure in facilitating the reintegration of former fighters into their local communities, and that has played a major role in ensuring peace and stability in the country.

7.6 Summary and Recommendations

The chapter has critically examined the roles of some important multilateral agencies, governments and community- based organizations in post-conflict peace building efforts in Liberia and Sierra Leone. It also discussed the background to the involvement of these international actors in post-conflict peace building initiatives in both countries. Some of the major problems encountered in the process have also been highlighted.

One of the major arguments put forward in the chapter is that international actors, including multilateral agencies and foreign governments seeking to promote post-conflict peace building efforts in both Liberia and Sierra Leone, should work closely with local agencies and initiatives rather than attempting to impose solutions from the outside, to ensure the success of post war peace-building efforts in both countries. Accordingly, it is suggested here that aid agencies and donor governments should increase their support for ECOWAS and the Mano River Union communities' efforts which are aimed at restoring lasting peace and stability not only in the two countries directly, but also in the sub-region at large. The chapter noted that since diverse and complex factors propelled the conflicts in West Africa, as in many other parts of the world, post-conflict peace building strategies should make use of diverse actors including civil society groups, religious leaders, women's and youth's groups, government officials and members of the international community, in post conflict reconstruction and reconciliation efforts and programmes if the peace is to last and be sustained.

Some of the problems and constraints of multilateral agencies in the peace-building activities include lack of effective co-ordination with local institutions and other key actors; inadequate knowledge and understanding of local conditions and the late provision of the necessary logistic and financial resources coupled with their rather limited mandates. In order to be successful, post-conflict peace building efforts by multilateral agencies, foreign governments and community-based organizations in Liberia and Sierra Leone must address these important issues:

- They must endeavour to address the root causes of the conflicts through initiatives designed to promote good governance, avoid economic deprivation/marginalization and political as well as social exclusion.
- Serious and determined efforts should be made to conveniently merge appropriate western post-conflict peace building methods with their relevant African counterparts

- There is an urgent need to strengthen post -conflict peace building capacities of the MRU and ECOWAS in the sub-region.
- Effective coordination of the efforts of all national and international actors in post conflict peace building in both countries.
- Foreign and local support should be directed towards rebuilding structures and systems that will serve all groups and communities rather than those that serve just one or a few groups.
- Providing employment opportunities for young men and women who may be enticed into taking up arms once again and fuel the conflict.
- International actors must adopt a sub-regional approach to peace building rather than trying to deal with each conflict separately in West Africa.
- There must be political will to provide timely and adequate funding for programmes that will facilitate and consolidate peace-building initiatives in war torn societies, including those of Liberia and Sierra Leone.
- Urgent steps must be taken to restructure and retrain the security agencies /forces to make them more efficient, transparent and ac-countable to elected political authority and the people at large

Notes and References

1. Richards, P. (1996), **Fighting for the Rain Forest: War, Youth and Resources in Sierra Leone**, Oxford: IAT, James Currey and Heinemann.
2. For more on this phenomenon, see Sesay, A. (1980), "Societal In-equities, Ethnic Heterogeneity and Political Instability. The case of Liberia", in *Plural Societies*, autumn, 1980, 15-30. Ahmadu Sesay (1983), "The Liberian Revolution, Forward March; Stop: About Faceturn", in *Conflict Quarterly*, Vol. 1, No. 4, Summer
3. Davies, Victor, A.B., 2000, "Sierra Leone: Ironic Tragedy" , *Journal of African Economies*, volume 9, number 3. Pp.350 .

4. Programme Support Document for Peace, Reconciliation, Rehabilitation and Reconstruction for Sierra Leone, SIL/97/o66A/01/31' GOSL/UNDP, pp.3

5. Al-Hassan, Conteh et al. 1999, in **Comprehending and Mastering Conflict**, London and New York: Zed Books.

6. Programme Support Document for Peace, Reconciliation and Reconstruction for Sierra Leone, ibid; 19

7. Aning, Kwesi Emmanuel, 1999, 'From eco-pessimism to eco-optimism: ECOMOG and West African Integration Process', *African Journal of Political Science*, Volume 4 No1, pp.29.

8. UNDP Programme support Document for peace, Reconciliation, Rehabilitation and Reconstruction in Sierra Leone, (Sil/97/006A/01? 31, July 1997 pp.19

9. Adeniji, Oluyemi, 2001, 'Conflict Resolution in Sierra Leone: The international Perspective' Paper presented at Second Annual Faculty Week Celebrations, Fourah Bay College, February 26, 3.

10. UNDP Programme support Document for peace, Reconciliation, Rehabilitation and Reconstruction in Sierra Leone, (Sil/97/006A/01? 31, July 1997 p.19

11. Aning, Kwesi Emmanuel, 1999, 'From eco-pessimism to eco-optimism: ECOMOG and West African Integration Process', *African Journal of Political Science*, Volume 4 No1, pp.29.

12. *Africa Recovery*, August 1998, pp. 29

Appendix 1

Executive Secretariat

National Committee for Disarmament, Demobilization and Reintegration (NCDDR)
Briefing Note: Status of Disarmament and Demobilization in Phase II
(Updated Monday, September 24, 2001)

Fighting Force	Disarmed			Demobilized			Discharged
	Children	Adults	Total	Children	Adults	Total	Total
CDF	1419	5118	6537	1327	4213	5540	5075
RUF	1276	9661	10937	1181	8434	9615	9488
EX-AFRC/EX-SLA	11	244	255	9	237	246	243
Other groups	21	44	65	19	30	49	41
Grand Total	2727	15067	17794	2536	12914	15450	14847

Appendix 2: Disarmed Personnel and Weapons Collected

Grand Total	Disarmed Personnel				Collected Weapons and Ammunition			
	RUF	CDF	Others	Total	Personal	Assault	Group op.	Ammunition
Bo	0	0	0	0	0	0	0	0
Bombali	379	5	2	386	11	102	2	1079
Bonthe	0	1233	13	1246	63	1920	10	2681
Freetown	144	313	133	590	11	367	4	1045
Kailahon	277	479	7	763	75	916	7	11565
Kenema	194	54	2	250	7	85	3	159
Koinadugu	288	845	9	1142	0	2	1	0
Kone	3726	2255	38	6019	1893	2102	0	144005
Moyamba	2	1740	13	1756	17	599	21	5
Port Loko/Kambia	1061	3386	98	4545	529	2274	50	103730
Pujehun	0	0	0	0	0	0	0 •	0
Tonkolili	466	627	5	1098	74	527	8	17886
Other Locations/NA	0	0	0	0	0	0	0	0
Grand Total	6537	10937	320	17794	2680	8894	106	282155

Note : All the figures are based on actual registration forms received from UNAMSIL and processed by the NCDDR. Report is prepared by the monitoring and Evaluation Unit of the Executive Secretariat of the NCDDR. 24/09/01

Chapter Eight: Conclusion
Amadu Sesay

This book is the outcome of a project on Civil Wars, Child Soldiers and Post Conflict Peace-building in Liberia and Sierra. It is concerned with three broad but intricately interwoven issues in the West African sub-region in the late 1980s and throughout the whole decade of the 1990s, State disintegration and civil war, child soldiers and post conflict peace building, and the reconstruction initiatives in Liberia and Sierra Leone.

The break down of state authority, and ultimately the civil wars in Liberia and Sierra Leone have been traced to several important factors. Significantly, both countries were the victims of political domination and marginalization by a small clique of political elites, coupled with gross economic mismanagement and widespread corruption. The phenomena reached a climax in the 1980s with the emergence of Master Sergeant Samuel Doe in Liberia following the bloody coup d'etat of April 12, 1980. His ruthless elimination of tne core of the men that carried out the coup, the ethnic coloration of his politics and mismanagement of the economy provided the backdrop for the open challenge that was posed to his regime by Charles Taylor, erstwhile Director of the powerful General Services Agency, GSA, in Doe's government.

In neighbouring Sierra Leone, the emergence of the All peoples' Congress, APC, under the leadership of Siaka Stevens ushered in a period of unprecedented corruption, ineptitude and crass economic mismanagement and indeed, ethnically centred governance. The situation was compounded by the appointment of handpicked successor, erstwhile Force Commander, Joseph Momoh, in 1985. The administration of Momoh left the country literally rudderless, as the new president did not seem to have any idea on how to run a government not to talk of managing a country. The breakout of the civil war in neighbouring Liberia in 1989 led to the

215

flight of hundreds of thousands of Liberian refugees into Sierra Leone and put a lot of pressure on the neglected and already overstretched social services and infrastructure. The inability of the Sierra Leone government to monitor or restrict the activities of the politically conscious refugees in part encourage the formation of a rival rebel movement in the country, ULIMO, which was to challenge the supremacy of the rival NPFL of Charles Taylor, a development that enraged him so much so that he did not hesitate to encourage dissident Sierra Leoneans led by a disgraced army corporal, Foday Sankoh, to start a war in Sierra Leone in March 1991. Of course, the literature on the war in Liberia and Sierra Leone is far from categorical as to the causes. That much came out clearly in the extensive review of the literature by Sesay and Ismail in Chapter One. Celestine Bassey in his excellent chapter on "The Nature and Dynamics of Civil Wars in West Africa", takes up the issue again, but this time with a West Africa focus.

It was clear from the on set that Doe and Momoh could not contain the rebel war effectively. Besides, both rebels and government forces in the two countries also engaged in large scale and unprecedented atrocities against the civilian populations. The two wars were also characterized by large-scale and unprecedented use of children as soldiers, the so-called 'child' or 'baby' soldiers, although the two countries were signatories to International Conventions banning the use of under aged children in combat. This phenomenon is the subject of Chapter Three by Amadu Sesay and Wale Ismail. They highlighted the indiscriminate use of children in the wars and the atrocities, which they were sometimes made to commit: murder, rape, impunity, and destruction of property and crude amputation of limbs especially in Sierra Leone. The barbarity of the war in Sierra Leone shocked the world and led to calls for those involved to be tried for war crimes and crimes against humanity. The end of the war in 2001 ultimately led to the establishment of an International War Crimes Tribunal in the country in 2002. The Tribunal swung into action in 2003 with the indictment of former warlord Foday Sankoh, former minister of Interior and erstwhile leader of the Kamajor militias, Hinga Norman. Another significant move by the Tribunal was the indictment and the warrant for the arrest of President Charles Taylor of Liberia while he was attending a peace conference at Akosombo, Ghana, in early June 2003.

The outbreak of the civil wars in Liberia and Sierra Leone was in part an indication of the failure of the Mano River Union, which had been put in place in 1973 by Presidents Siaka Stevens of Sierra Leone and his Liberian counterpart, William Tolbert. Guinea was to join the organization a decade later in 1983. Ironically, the Mano River Union, an enterprise that was ostensibly designed to promote good neighbourliness and development in the member states, became instead, a victim of misrule and political instability. Guinea, the third leg of the trilateral politico-economic union bore a lot of the brunt of the wars not only by way of the massive inflow of refugees from both countries into its territory, but also through the destabilization policies embarked upon by Charles Taylor even after the Liberian war had formally come to end in 1997. These and other important issues are the subject of two insightful chapters by Charles Ukeje; "State Disintegration and Civil War in Liberia", and "Sierra Leone: The Long Dissent into Civil War".

In "State Disintegration and Civil War in Liberia", Ukeje traced both the historical and contemporary factors that led to the break down of state authority and ultimately the civil war in 1989. He also critically examined the tortuous road to peace in that country covering the efforts of ECOWAS which put in place an unprecedented regional peace keeping force, ECOMOG, to bring the war to an end. He noted that the refusal of the United States, former provider and protector of the Liberian state, was a fall out of the end of the ideological rivalry between the former Soviet Union and the United States of America. For according to Ukeje, Liberia lost its pride of place and geo-strategic importance soon after the end of the Cold War. Although 'peace' was restored in Liberia after almost eight years of bloody civil war, Ukeje concluded that "even an arm-chair observer of the political landscape in post-war Liberia cannot be fooled into believing that the country would enjoy a durable peace for too long". His conclusion turned out to be extremely prophetic as Liberia is facing yet another round of war brought about by a new rebel movement, Liberians united for Reconstruction and Democracy, LURD, challenging Charles Taylor's regime.

Sierra Leone gained notoriety in the 1990s as a result of its brutal civil war, which lasted for a decade. Not only were thousands of civilians killed in that war, thousands of others were also the victims of rape, slave labour and crude amputations. Indeed, it was the later that caught the imagination of the global community culminating in the setting of the International War Crimes Tribunal in Freetown. In "Sierra Leone: The long Descent to Civil War", Charles Ukeje gave a refreshing and welcome interpretation and analysis of the events that led to, as well as the course of what he called the "uncivil war". He argues convincingly, that "…the roles of external forces particularly those of Charles Taylor of Liberia, only gives a partial, incomplete explanation of the genesis and trajectory of the civil war in Sierra Leone". His conclusion is that stakeholders that were both internal and external facilitated the tortuous peace process in the country. Of particular interest was the keen interest that Britain, the erstwhile colonial power, took in ending the "uncivil war ", including the deployment of its special forces in the country. That singular act, above all, made the difference in the difficult search for peace in the country.

The rest of the book tackled issues, which have so far not received the attention they deserve from West African scholars. Chapter Five by Osman Gbla of Fourah Bay College, Sierra Leone, examined "Post War Trauma Among Child Soldiers in Liberia and Sierra Leone," which he described as the "unenviable legacy" of child soldiers in the civil wars in both countries. He regretted that although their war time experiences either as victims or as perpetrators of atrocities, traumatized them in diverse ways, no consistent effort has been made particularly in Liberia, to de-traumatize and reintegrate the former "baby soyas" into civil society for productive post conflict engagements. He also cautioned that even where it is done, methods of treating post war trauma in child soldiers do have limitations that must be taken into consideration by post conflict regimes and agencies interested in reintegrating them into civil society. Osman concluded his rather pioneering chapter with several important recommendations, among which are the following: since the family and community are very essential components of civil society in both Liberia and Sierra Leone, they should be empowered to enhance the social acceptance and tolerance of former child soldiers; "given the devastating impact of the two civil wars on girls and thousands of disabled children, post conflict trauma healing, rehabilitation and reintegration programmes should endeavour to incorporate their special needs in terms of health and medical care, education, counseling and protection from societal rejection".

Osman in the final section of the book takes up the role(s) of multilateral agencies in post conflict peace building. Again this is another important issue that has not received the deserved attention from the academia. He argued that given the devastation of the civil wars in Liberia and Sierra Leone and the interrelatedness of the countries of the West African sub-region, especially those in the Mano River zone, multilateral agencies interested in post conflict peace-building "must galvanize efforts that would also ensure sub-regional peace" and stability. Expectedly, most of the agencies that are involved in post conflict reconstruction and peace building in the two countries are mainly external to the sub-region: United Nations agencies, the World Bank, the IMF and refreshingly, the African Development Bank, ADB. As for so-called friendly governments, Britain seemed to be playing the most critical and leading roles in post conflict peace building especially in Sierra Leone, than any other. Unfortunately, the same cannot be said of the role of the United States of America, Liberia's erstwhile "step-father" in the post conflict peace building efforts in that country. That neglect, in large measure, also explains the relapse into another round of rebel war and the unprecedented suffering inflicted not only on its people but also to those in neighbouring Sierra Leone and Guinea.

What has come out clearly in all the chapters in the book are the lingering effects of both the colonial and post colonial experiences of not only Liberia and Sierra Leone but all African states in general. This is true of Cote d'Ivoire, which was once considered as the haven of prosperity and stability on the West African coast. The descent of that francophone country into chaos and disintegration culminating in a bloody civil war and contest for power between the North and South, since 2001 is clear testimony to the fact that the veneer of prosperity and unity merely existed because of the 'cover' provided by the Cold War environment. Thus, it is now clear that the so-called Cold War was, for some parts of the world, not cold after all. Not only that, its impacts have had a longer term effect particularly on the peripheries of global politics which are also the ones that are ill-equipped to cope with its consequences. For while the chief Cold War warrior, the United States of America and its west European allies were quick in restoring law and order in the former communist states of Eastern Europe, they have not been so enthusiastic in responding to the dire needs of countries in other parts of the world and most especially, those in Africa. This is to be expected, since the Cold War premium that was placed on African countries also evaporated with its end. Thus, Liberia, once considered an important Cold War listening and spying out-post for America, could be easily and rather callously disowned after the war by Washington D.C as "an African problem that required an African response". In that regard, the French and the British tend to have a better track record in post Cold War West African politics. The French have been very much involved in restoring peace and stability in Cote d'Ivoire including the deployment of French troops in that country to separate the warring factions, and in hosting several peace talks aimed at bringing lasting peace to that country. Britain, as pointed out earlier, extended the same 'courtesy' to Sierra Leone during and after its most difficult years.

Thus, and in spite of all its failings, the response of the Economic Community of West African States, ECOWAS, to the two civil wars must be commended. For many years, its intervention force, ECOMOG, remained the only hope to the people of Sierra Leone and Liberia in their most desperate hours, the bridge between hope and total despair. In both Liberia and Sierra Leone, the popular refrain is: "Thank God for ECOMOG". And in a bitter twist of irony, some West African leaders who were vilified at home became instant heroes in the two countries. The lessons that must be learned from the civil wars and the intervention of ECOWAS are that there is no alternative in the end, to good governance, transparency and accountability at home. Leaders must always, first and foremost, endeavour to cater for the needs of their entire population and not sections of it. They must also be reminded that corruption does empower but such empowerment is transient. As the Liberian and Sierra Leonean experiences clearly demonstrate in West Africa, the consequences could be devastating for their teeming citizens. These are some of the enduring lessons that we have learned from the experiences in Liberia and Sierra Leone over the last decade and a half. Another lesson that we have learned from Liberia and Sierra Leone's experiences is that there is no alternative, in the final analysis; to self-help especially when it is credible. The ECOWAS interventions in Liberia and Sierra Leone are thus very encouraging from such a perspective. More importantly, is the fact that West African leaders were themselves able to learn bitter lessons from the misadventure-although putting their houses in order is another thing entirely! -

There are prospects for improvement, nevertheless. The first hope results from the creation of a unified conflict management mechanism for the sub-region. The mechanism has been backed up by the establishment of listening posts in several parts of the sub-region to act as early warning systems and to facilitate, ultimately, the prevention and management of conflicts when they do break out. Apart from these military mechanisms, ECOWAS has also been trying to consolidate on the economic front. While that is still wobbly for obvious reasons, there is no gainsaying the fact that salvation for the member countries in a globalized world lies in closer sub-regional cooperation and integration. But of course, economic integration cannot be realized in an atmosphere of political instability and blood shed. This is an issue that also caught the attention of the Community and was given practical expression in 2000 when a group of experts met for two weeks in the Senegalese capital, Dakar, to fashion out a **Protocol on Democracy and Good Governance** (henceforth simply the Protocol), for the sub-region. The document is important not only because it was unprecedented, but also because it was the result of a realization that political convergence is an indispensable ingredient for sub-regional political stability and economic integration.

Long before the protocol was signed in 2000, the Community had put in place other confidence building measures among the Member States. The 1978 Protocol on Non-Aggression and the 1981 Protocol Relating to Mutual Assistance on Defence[1] are clear examples of the determination of West African leaders to take care of the confidence building measures that were put in place in the early years of the Community. Finally, in 1999, ECOWAS once again embarked upon another important conflict prevention and management enterprise, when it adoption the Protocol Relating to the Mechanism for Conflict Prevention, Management, Resolution, Peace keeping and Security. However, the Protocol on Democracy and Good Governance is certainly the "latest and most far reaching attempt by ECOWAS to consolidate peace, security and stability in a sub-region that witnessed two violent and even notorious civil wars within a decade".[2] The Protocol is important because it has the potential of impacting "directly and indirectly on the ordinary man in ECOWAS Member States, thereby enhancing sub-regional peace, security, stability and economic development". Besides, it also raises the possibility of "redeeming the battered image of the sub-region" during the brutal civil wars in Liberia and Sierra Leone. The Protocol is divided into three very broad chapters: Chapter 1 deals with the Principles; Chapter 2 is on the Modalities for Implementation, which Chapter 3 deals with the General and Final Provisions. In all, the document has eight sections each of which is devoted to a topical issue in the political landscape of the sub-region. For example, Section 1 deals with the 'Constitutional Convergence Principles' in all the Partner States, while Section 11 is on 'Elections.' It is significant to note that the organization and conduct of elections have been divisive issues in many states of the sub-region that have contributed to political instability and violence in those states in particular and the sub-region in general[3].

Thus, it is hoped that the adoption of this wide raging Protocol would bring about the desired and well-deserved peace and stability in the sub-region. For it is only in an atmosphere of peace that the laudable and indispensable goal of sub-regional economic integration would take place. The successful conduct of general elections in Nigeria in April 2003 and the installation of another civil regime under Olusegun Obasanjo broke the jinx of civilian to civilian transition in Nigeria, Africa's budding super power. What is needed, all the same, is for the international community to give its support to these important moves which are designed to end the bitter experiences of the immediate post Cold War era in the sub-region, and put in place mechanisms and measures that would enhance cooperation, peace and stability in West Africa and a better life for its teeming citizens who are at the moment among the most deprived and poorest of the world's population. Several important questions immediately beg for answers: would Nigeria, other West African leaders and political elite continue in this preferred path diligently and for how long? Would the international community put its money where its mouth is? Time will tell.

Notes and References

1. Amadu Sesay (2002), "The Role of ECOWAS in Promoting Peace and Security in West Africa", in DPMN Bulletin, Addis Ababa, Vol. 1X, No. 3, June 2002, 21

2. Ibid; 22. For more on this, see, **Treaty of the Economic Community of West Africa, ECOWAS; Protocol on Democracy and Good Governance Supplementary to the Protocol Relating to the Mechanism for Conflict Prevention, Management, Resolution, Peace Keeping and Security**, Abuja: ECOWAS Secretariat, 1999; Amadu Sesay (1999), "Between the Olive Branch and the AK47: Paradoxes of Recent Military Interventions in West Africa", ISSUP Bulletin, 6/99, University of Pretoria, and Amadu Sesay (2000), "West African Military Interventions in the 1990s: The Case of ECOWAS in Liberia and Sierra Leone", in L. Du Plessis and M. Hough (eds.), **Managing African Conflicts: The Challenge of Military Intervention**, Pretoria: Human Sciences Research Council and CEMIS.

3. The conduct of elections and post election arguments and disagreements have been the bane of many West African States, most especially Nigeria, the most populous and powerful state in the sub-region and the driving force behind ECOWAS. The successful conduct of the April 2003 elections and the return of Obasanjo as president have given some hope that once and for all, the jinx has been broken and that the military will forever remain in the barracks.

Amadu Sesay is project coordinator and Head, Department of International Relations, Obafemi Awolowo University, Ile-Ife, Nigeria.

Celestine Bassey is Professor and Head, Department of Political Science, University Of Calabar, Calabar, Nigeria

Charles Ukeje is a lecturer in the Department of International Relations, Obafemi Awolowo University, Ile-Ife, Nigeria.

Osman Gbla is lecturer in the Department of Political Science, Fourah Bay College, University of Sierra Leone, Freetown, Sierra Leone.

Wale Ismail is a research student in the Department of Peace Studies, University of Bradford, United Kingdom. He was a Research Assistant at the Stockholm International Peace Research Institute, SIPRI in 2002.